THE ELECTORAL COLLEGE

FAILURES OF ORIGINAL INTENT AND A PROPOSED CONSTITUTIONAL AMENDMENT FOR DIRECT POPULAR VOTE

ALAN E. JOHNSON

Philosophia Publications
Pittsburgh, Pennsylvania

Copyright © 2018 by Alan E. Johnson

For permissions or other information, contact Alan E. Johnson at alanjohnson10@comcast.net

Print ISBN: 978-0-692-07832-7
Digital ISBN: 978-0-692-07950-8
Library of Congress Control Number: 2018935460

Published by
Philosophia Publications
2400 Oxford Dr., # 112
Pittsburgh, PA 15102
412-498-2997
http://www.PhilosophiaPublications.com
http://www.Facebook.com/philosophiapublications

For Bob

Some men look at constitutions with sanctimonious reverence, and deem them like the arc of the covenant, too sacred to be touched. They ascribe to the men of the preceding age a wisdom more than human, and suppose what they did to be beyond amendment. I knew that age well; I belonged to it, and labored with it. It deserved well of its country. It was very like the present, but without the experience of the present; and forty years of experience in government is worth a century of book-reading; and this they would say themselves, were they to rise from the dead. I am certainly not an advocate for frequent and untried changes in laws and constitutions. I think moderate imperfections had better be borne with; because, when once known, we accommodate ourselves to them, and find practical means of correcting their ill effects. But I know also, that laws and institutions must go hand in hand with the progress of the human mind. As that becomes more developed, more enlightened, as new discoveries are made, new truths disclosed, and manners and opinions change with the change of circumstances, institutions must advance also, and keep pace with the times. We might as well require a man to wear still the coat which fitted him when a boy, as civilized society to remain ever under the regimen of their barbarous ancestors.

—Letter of Thomas Jefferson to Samuel Perceval, July 12, 1816

Contents

PREFACE

During the late evening and early morning hours of November 8-9, 2016, it became clear that presidential candidate Hillary Rodham Clinton had prevailed in the popular vote over her opponent, Donald J. Trump. It also became clear that Trump would win a majority of votes in the Electoral College and thus be sworn into office as the new president on January 20, 2017. And he was.

When all the numbers were added up, Clinton had beaten Trump in the popular election by a plurality of 2,868,691 votes. Trump nevertheless became president by winning 304 of 538 electoral votes; he needed only 270.

The 2016 election was a reprise, on steroids, of the 2000 presidential election. In 2000, George W. Bush squeaked by in the Electoral College with 271 votes—one vote more than the 270 needed. Al Gore had, however, won a plurality of 543,895 nationwide popular votes over Bush. It was a close election, decided when the U.S. Supreme Court ordered a halt to the Florida recount. With Florida in his pocket, Bush obtained enough electoral votes to win the Electoral College and thus the presidency.

Like many Americans, I basically shrugged off the outcome of the 2000 election. After all, Bush and Gore were both mainstream candidates with previous political experience. They were both supported widely by their respective political parties. It turned out that Bush governed differently from the "compassionate conservative" image he projected in the election, but we did not know that then. During the election campaign he somehow seemed like a moderate, especially when compared with the more incendiary voices in his political party.

The 2016 election was different. For the first time in American history, a candidate with no former political or military experience won the presidency. That candidate was a celebrity with a history of making statements that could be—and were—interpreted as being racist, xenophobic, misogynistic, and authoritarian. Many of those statements were made during the 2016 campaign itself. Although the voters had rejected Trump by almost three million votes, the Electoral College anointed him president. What did such a result imply about the nature of the Electoral College? Why indeed had the American founders instituted such a counterintuitive system more than two centuries ago?

These questions led me to an immediate investigation of the origins and history of the Electoral College. I soon decided to write a book about this institution and possible alternatives to it. I thought I would write the book in a handful of months. It took me more than a year. I discovered that the origins of the Electoral College were more complicated than what is often represented today. I wanted to get the history right. And that inquiry turned out to be quite fascinating. Additionally, I found the various positions taken over the decades and centuries about the Electoral College to be perplexing. I needed to sort them out and understand them on their own terms before making my own evaluation.

The present book is the result of all this research and analysis. The first thing I wrote was the lengthy Appendix entitled "A Detailed Narrative of the Debates on the Selection of the President in the 1787 Constitutional Convention." That chronological discussion provided the groundwork for all that followed. Chapter 1 treats some of the same material topically in a discussion of the intentions of the framers of the Electoral College. Chapter 2 examines the understandings of the ratifiers of the Electoral College. Chapter 3 surveys the early frustration of original intent in the operation of the Electoral College from 1789 through the ratification of the Twelfth Amendment in 1804. Chapter 4 discusses the failures of original intent from the Twelfth Amendment to the present, including the critical elections of 2000 and 2016. Chapter 5 evaluates the current operation of the winner-take-all Electoral College and explains why—contrary to the mantra of many of its defenders—it is essentially different from the Electoral College conceived by the American founders. That chapter also analyzes and evaluates the major alternatives, other than direct popular vote, that have been proposed to today's Electoral College. Finally, Chapter 6 sets forth the legal text of a proposed constitutional amendment for direct popular vote with instant runoff voting and explains, in layperson's language, what those provisions mean. It also discusses the advantages of such a system and responds to anticipated criticisms of the proposed amendment.

Article V of the Constitution dictates the procedure for adoption of a constitutional amendment. Absent a new constitutional convention (which has never happened and is unlikely to happen), two-thirds of each house of Congress must approve a proposed amendment, and three-fourths of the states must ratify it. Considering the political climate of the United States in recent decades, the proposed amendment will not be adopted in my lifetime. This is one of several reasons I have dedicated this book to my son. Perhaps this needed reform will occur within his lifetime.

As always, I wish to thank my wife, Mimi, who kindly reviewed the manuscript of this book for readability and style and whose suggestions I have substantially adopted.

Supplemental comments and errata, if any, to this book will   be   posted at https://chicago.academia.edu/AlanJohnson.

CHAPTER 1: THE INTENTIONS OF THE FRAMERS OF THE ELECTORAL COLLEGE

Delegates to the 1787 Constitutional Convention in Philadelphia were not of one mind about the issue of presidential selection. They participated in debates and voted intermittently on various competing methods for selecting the president during the entire period of the Convention before finally deciding on the Electoral College.[1] Near the end of the proceedings, which lasted from May 25 through September 17, 1787, Pennsylvania delegate James Wilson acknowledged: "This subject has greatly divided the House, and will also divide people out of doors [the public]. It is in truth the most difficult of all on which we have had to decide."[2]

The United States had declared its independence from Great Britain in July of 1776. From that time until 1781, the management of the War for Independence and a few other general concerns were performed by an ad hoc entity called the Continental Congress. In 1777, the Continental Congress proposed a written constitution called the Articles of Confederation. It was not until March 1, 1781, however, that all thirteen states ratified that document, thereby making it legally effective under its terms.[3]

The Articles of Confederation, like the predecessor Continental Congress, had a unicameral legislature called the Congress (sometimes referred to as the Confederation Congress), in which each state had one vote. The Congress alone had both legislative and executive powers. Although Congress elected presidents (presiding officers over their proceedings), the separation of powers embodied in the 1787 Constitution was "unknown to the Congress of the pre-Confederation or Confederation years." No separate executive branch of government existed. The Congress established offices of secretary for foreign affairs, superintendent of finance, secretary of war, and secretary of marine in early 1781, but these officers all reported directly to Congress.[4]

On February 21, 1787, the Confederation Congress resolved that "in the opinion of Congress it is expedient that on the second Monday in May next a Convention of delegates who shall have been appointed by the several states be held at Philadelphia **for the sole and express purpose of revising the Articles of Confederation** and reporting to Congress and the several [state] legislatures such alterations and provisions therein as shall when agreed to in Congress and confirmed by the states **render the federal constitution adequate to the exigencies of Government & the preservation of the Union.**"[5] When the Constitutional Convention met, it was decided that each state would have only one vote in the proceedings, even though the respective states had each appointed more than one delegate to the Convention. A majority of the delegates from each state would determine that state's votes. In the event of a tie or the absence of a quorum in the delegation, the state's vote would not be counted.[6]

Historians use the term "framers" to refer to the delegates who attended the Constitutional Convention. The Appendix to this book contains a detailed chronological narrative of their debates and votes on the question of the method of electing the president. This chapter, instead of proceeding chronologically, explains the various views of the framers on the alternative modes of presidential selection; it also surveys the major developments leading to the final Electoral College provisions in the 1787 Constitution. The next chapter discusses such issues as they arose in the ratification debates after the Constitution was sent to the state conventions for their consideration and decisions on ratification. The 1787 Constitution was ratified by the requisite number of states in 1788, and the new government went into operation in 1789.

All dates referring to the Convention's proceedings occurred in the year 1787. The delegates did not at first use the terms "president," "House of Representatives," or "Senate." Instead, they spoke of the "executive," the "first house," and the "second house," respectively.

Most of the quotations in this chapter are from the famous notes of James Madison, taken in rough form at the Constitutional Convention and somewhat later (usually within two or three days) refined by him into the notes that have gone down in history as our best source of the debates in the Convention. I follow the practice of editor Max Farrand in enclosing Madison's later revisions of his notes in angle brackets (< >).[7]

3

ADVOCATES AND OPPONENTS OF DIRECT POPULAR ELECTION OF THE PRESIDENT

James Wilson, a Pennsylvania delegate who later became a Supreme Court justice, was one of the strongest advocates of the direct popular election of the national executive, later called the "president." At the beginning of deliberations, on May 30, Wilson said he favored "an appointment by the people. He wished to derive not only both branches of the [national] Legislature from the people, without the intervention of the State Legislatures <but the Executive also;> in order to make them as independent as possible of each other, as well as of the States."[8] On July 24, after much debate over the mode of electing the executive, Wilson said that "[h]is opinion remained unshaken that we ought to resort to the people for the election."[9]

Pennsylvania delegate Gouverneur Morris also strongly advocated popular election of the national executive. On July 17, he stated:

> [The national executive] ought to be elected by the people at large, by the freeholders of the Country. That difficulties attend this mode, he admits. But they have been found superable in N.Y. & in [Connecticut] and would he believed be found so, in the case of an Executive for the U. States. If the people should elect, they will never fail to prefer some man of distinguished character, or services: some man, if he might so speak, of continental reputation.[10]

Morris's reference to New York can be explained by the fact that "New York's 1777 constitution was the first to have the governor elected by direct popular vote."[11] Connecticut's governor was also elected by the people.[12]

On July 19, Morris remarked:

> It is necessary that the Executive Magistrate should be the guardian of the people, even of the lower classes, agst. Legislative tyranny, against the Great & the wealthy who in the course of things will necessarily compose—the Legislative body. Wealth tends to corrupt the mind & to nourish its love of power, and to stimulate it to oppression. History proves this to be the spirit of the opulent. . . . The Executive therefore ought to be so constituted as to be the great protector of the Mass of the people.[13]

Similarly, Massachusetts delegate Rufus King "was much disposed to think that . . . the people at large would chuse wisely. There was indeed some difficulty arising from the improbability of a general concurrence of the people in favor of one man. On the whole, he was of opinion that an appointment by electors chosen by the people for the purpose, would be liable to fewest objections."[14] At the time of the Constitutional Convention, the delegates had no inkling of the possibility of national political parties that would each nominate a presidential candidate. If people had a direct vote, the ballots they would be given would not have the preprinted

5

names of a few presidential candidates on them. Instead, the voters would write in the names of the persons they personally favored for the presidency. Under this system, there would be a large number of presidential candidates, probably without any one of them receiving a majority of the votes cast. This would especially be true, many delegates thought, because voters would tend to vote for someone they knew, or knew of, in their own state. In response to the argument that a majority of the voters would never agree on one candidate, James Wilson stated that "the concurrence of a majority of people is not a necessary principle of election, nor required as such in any of the States. But allowing the objection all its force, it may be obviated by the expedient used in [Massachusetts] where the Legislature by majority of voices, decide in case a majority of people do not concur in favor of one of the candidates. This would restrain the choice to a good nomination at least, and prevent in a great degree intrigue & cabal."[15]

James Madison of Virginia also expressed support for direct popular election of the national executive, while noting some problems he perceived in that procedure. On July 19, he stated:

> **The people at large was in his opinion the fittest in itself. It would be as likely as any that could be devised to produce an Executive Magistrate of distinguished Character.** The people generally could only know & vote for some Citizen whose merits had rendered him an

6

object of general attention & esteem. There was one difficulty however of a serious nature attending an immediate choice by the people. **The right of suffrage was much more diffusive in the Northern than the Southern States; and the latter could have no influence in the election on the score of the Negroes. The substitution of electors obviated this difficulty and seemed on the whole to be liable to the fewest objections.**[16]

On July 25, after the Convention had rejected an electoral college concept, Madison said:

The remaining mode was an election by the people or rather by the <qualified part of them> at large. With all its imperfections he liked this best. He would not repeat either the general argumts. for or the objections agst this mode. He would only take notice of two difficulties which he admitted to have weight. The first arose from the disposition in the people to prefer a Citizen of their own State, and the disadvantage this wd. throw on the smaller States. Great as this objection might be he did not think it equal to such as lay agst. every other mode which had been proposed. He thought too that some expedient might be hit upon that would obviate it. The second difficulty arose from the disproportion of <qualified voters> in

7

the N. & S. States, and the disadvantages which this mode would throw on the latter. The answer to this objection was: 1. that this disproportion would be continually decreasing under the influence of the Republican laws introduced in the S. States, and the more rapid increase of their population, 2. That local considerations must give way to the general interest. As an individual from the S. States he was willing to make the sacrifice.[17]

In the July 25 notes, Madison later replaced his original word "freeholders" with "qualified part of them [the people]" and, in the second instance of "freeholders," with the language "qualified part." All states existing at the time of the Convention had property qualifications for voting.[18] Slaves could not vote. With one notable exception, neither northern nor southern states allowed women to vote.[19] And some states "denied the vote to large numbers of white males because of church affiliation."[20] Accordingly, all references in the Constitutional Convention and in other contemporaneous documents to election of the president (national executive) by "the people" must be understood to include only the "qualified voters" among the people.

In the final Constitution, the president was to be elected by electors appointed "in such Manner as the Legislature [of each state] shall direct" (Article II, Section 1, Clause 2). The legislature of each state appointed its two senators (Article I, Section 1, Clause 1, later changed by the Seventeenth Amendment in 1913 to election by the people of each state). In the Constitution, therefore, the national government had no occasion to define popular voting qualifications with regard to these offices. In contrast, Article I, Section 2, Clause 1 provided: "The House of Representatives shall be composed of Members chosen every second Year by the People of the several States, and the Electors in each State shall have the Qualifications requisite for Electors of the most numerous Branch of the State Legislature."

In the above-quoted excerpts from his July 19 and 25 speeches, Madison pointed to the disparity between the northern and southern states regarding their suffrage laws. The southern states did not, of course, permit their slaves to vote. Some of the northern states had enacted laws to abolish slavery—often a gradual emancipation over a period of time. In any event, slavery was much more prevalent in the southern than in the northern states.[21]

What were the electoral consequences of what Madison called the "more diffusive" suffrage in the northern states? If the president were to be elected by direct popular vote, only the actual voters—not slaves, women, or men of insufficient property—would count. In such case, the northern states would outvote the southern states. The "solution"—diabolical as it was—was to adopt an electoral system in which the slaves were counted in some manner in the apportionment of the numbers of electors among the states. The framework upon which the delegates eventually arrived was for electors, appointed in

9

such manner as each state legislature directed, to elect the president. The catch was that each state would be apportioned a number of electors that was the total of that state's representatives (in the House of Representatives) and senators. Each state had two senators in the final version of the Constitution, but each state was apportioned representatives in the House of Representatives on the basis of that state's total population, including three-fifths of its slaves. Accordingly, the Three-Fifths Clause of the Constitution ensured that the southern states would be dominant in presidential elections.[22] When Madison said on July 19 that "[t]he substitution of electors obviated [the] difficulty" of the large population of nonvoting slaves in the southern states, he was undoubtedly thinking of what became the Three-Fifths Clause of the Constitution. This three-fifths concept was being discussed by Convention delegates as early as May 21[23] and was adopted on July 12.[24]

It is unclear what exactly Madison's role in all of this was. Madison was known to express opposition to slavery, though he himself acquired slaves as a result of his family connections. Madison was a hard-headed realist. He knew that slavery was not going to disappear in his lifetime, and he was, after all, a delegate from a southern state. When he said on July 19 that "[t]he substitution of electors obviated this difficulty" of the northern states having a "more diffusive" suffrage, he was undoubtedly thinking ahead of the application of the Three-Fifths Compromise, adopted on July 12, to the apportionment of electors among the states. Coincidentally or not, North Carolina delegate Hugh Williamson proposed the very next day that electors for the national executive should be apportioned to each state in future elections on the basis of the allocation of representatives to such state in the first house (House of Representatives) of the legislature. In accordance with the July 12 Three-Fifths Compromise and the July 16 Great Compromise, this allocation of representatives was based on the nonslave population of the state (not including Native Americans not taxed) plus three-fifths of that state's slaves. Although Williamson's motion was not seconded and was not the subject of a vote, it became the kernel for the ultimate determination of this issue.[25]

On July 25, John Dickinson of Delaware stated that he "had long leaned towards an election [of the national executive] by the people which he regarded as the best and purest source." He was aware, however, of certain objections against popular election, especially from "the partiality of the States to their respective Citizens." But he thought this alleged vice could be turned into a virtue. "Let the people of each State chuse its best Citizen. The people will know the most eminent characters of their own States, and the people of different States will feel an emulation in selecting those of which they will have the greatest reason to be proud." Accordingly "[o]ut of the thirteen names thus selected, an Executive Magistrate may be chosen either by the Natl Legislature, or by Electors appointed by it."[26]

Finally, on August 24, Daniel Carroll of Maryland moved that the president "shall be elected by ballot by the people." James Wilson seconded the motion, but it failed by a vote of nine states to two. Only Pennsylvania and Delaware voted in the affirmative.[27]

In summary, James Wilson, Gouverneur Morris, and Daniel Carroll supported direct election of the president by the people. Rufus King, James Madison, and John Dickinson expressed support for popular election of the president but saw difficulties that they attempted to ameliorate by less than purely democratic means.

In contrast to these advocates of popular election, several delegates expressed strong opposition to the election of the national executive (president) by the people.

Elbridge Gerry of Massachusetts was one of the most vociferous opponents of popular election. On July 19, he claimed that "[t]he people are uninformed, and would be misled by a few designing men. . . . The popular mode of electing the chief Magistrate would certainly be the worst of all."[28] On July 25, he stated: "A popular election in this case is radically vicious. The ignorance of the people would put it in the power of some one set of men dispersed through the Union & acting in Concert to delude them into any appointment."[29]

Connecticut delegate Roger Sherman, a leader of the small-state caucus, thought that the people at large "will never be sufficiently informed of characters, and besides will never give a majority of votes to any one man. They will generally vote for some man in their own State, and the largest State will have the best chance for the appointment."[30]

South Carolina delegate Charles Pinckney dismissed an election by the people as "being liable to the most obvious and striking objections. They will be led by a few active & designing men. The most populous States by combining in favor of the same individual will be able to carry their points."[31] Gouverneur Morris replied: "It is said the people will be led by a few designing men. This might happen in a small district. It can never happen throughout the continent." In response to the argument that the people will be uninformed, Morris said that "they will not be uninformed of those great & illustrious characters which have merited their esteem & confidence."[32]

George Mason of Virginia remarked that "a Government which is to last ought at least to be practicable. Would this be the case if the proposed election should be left to the people at large[?] He conceived it would be as unnatural to refer the choice of a proper character for chief Magistrate to the people, as it would, to refer a trial of colours to a blind man. The extent of the Country renders it impossible that the people can have the requisite capacity to judge of the respective pretensions of the Candidates."[33]

Oliver Ellsworth of Connecticut thought that "[t]he objection drawn from the different sizes of the States, is unanswerable. The Citizens of the largest States would invariably prefer the Candidate within the State: and the largest States wd. invariably have the man."[34]

South Carolina delegate Pierce Butler argued that the government "should not be made so complex & unwieldy as to disgust the States. This would be the case, if the election shd. be referred to the people."[35]

Accordingly, Elbridge Gerry, Roger Sherman, Charles Pinckney, George Mason, Oliver Ellsworth, and Pierce Butler opposed direct popular election of the president. Their arguments generally were that the people were not qualified to choose the president, because they would be ignorant of the leading candidates or because they would be influenced by demagogic leaders or because they would usually vote for someone from their own state. The small-state caucus feared that the large states would dominate in presidential elections if those elections were determined by popular vote.

ADVOCATES AND OPPONENTS OF ELECTION OF THE PRESIDENT BY THE NATIONAL LEGISLATURE

The deliberations of the Constitutional Convention began with the presentation of what came to be called the "Virginia Plan" or the "Randolph resolutions." This was a sketch of a new constitution that had been drafted by the Virginia delegation at a time before a quorum of state delegations had arrived in Philadelphia. Edmund Randolph, the governor of Virginia, presented these resolutions to the Convention on May 29.[36]

The Virginia Plan proposed, among other things, that a national executive be instituted, to be chosen by the national legislature.[37] Most of the state governments

14

selected their governors (sometimes called "president") in this manner, and the concept was accordingly familiar to most of the delegates.[38] It was widely believed that making the national executive subservient to the national legislature would prevent the president from becoming a king. The Americans had, after all, fought a War for Independence in order to extricate themselves from the evils of monarchy and from a parliament corrupted by that monarchy. As Connecticut delegate Roger Sherman put it on June 1, "An independence of the Executive on [from] the supreme Legislative, was in his opinion the very essence of tyranny if there was any such thing."[39] Decades later, Thomas Jefferson remarked on the errors of such thinking during the founding era:

> The infancy of the subject at that moment, and our inexperience of self-government occasioned gross departures ... from genuine republican canons. In truth, the abuses of monarchy had so much filled all the space of political contemplation that we imagined every thing republican which was not monarchy. We had not yet penetrated to the mother-principle that 'governments are republican only in proportion as they embody the will of their people, and execute it.' Hence, our first constitutions had really no leading principle in them. But experience & reflection have but more & more confirmed me in the particular importance of the equal representation then proposed."[40]

The Virginia delegates proposed a bicameral legislature in which each house would be represented by population and not by state. What eventually became the House of Representatives was to be elected by the people, and what became the Senate was to be elected by the House of Representatives on the basis of nominations of candidates by the state legislatures. The number of delegates apportioned to each state in both houses of the national legislature would be proportional to "the Quotas of contribution [taxes], or to the number of free inhabitants, as the one or the other rule may seem best in different cases."[41]

The "Quotas of contribution" language was probably an implicit reference to what became the Three-Fifths Clause (Article I Section 2, Clause 3) of the 1787 Constitution: "**Representatives and direct Taxes shall be apportioned among the several States** which may be included within this Union, according to their respective Numbers, which shall be determined by adding to the whole Number of free Persons, including those bound to Service for a Term of Years, and excluding Indians not taxed, **three fifths of all other Persons** [slaves]." (Emphasis added.) Under the Virginia Plan, it seems implicit that the northern states would be apportioned legislative representatives on the basis of the number of each state's free inhabitants, whereas the southern states would be apportioned representatives on the basis of their respective numbers of free inhabitants plus three-fifths of their slaves. The Virginia Plan assumed that both houses of

16

Congress would be represented on the basis of population, as distinguished from equal state suffrage.

On June 15, William Paterson of New Jersey presented what is known as the New Jersey Plan. Unlike the Virginia Plan, this proposal was designed to modify, not replace, the Articles of Confederation. As such, it favored the small states. Like the Articles of Confederation, the New Jersey Plan retained the unicameral legislative body called the "Congress." Each state would continue to have only one vote in the Congress, though there could be several members of a particular state's delegation. Congress would, in turn, elect a national executive.[42]

Although many differences existed between the Virginia and the New Jersey proposals, they both agreed on the basic principle that the national legislature should elect the national executive. After considering various alternatives, the Convention returned to this default position again and again during the long history of the Philadelphia proceedings. Only near the end of the Convention did the delegates finally decide on an alternative procedure.

The following delegates to the Constitutional Convention expressed support for election of the national executive by the national legislature: Edmund Randolph (May 29, July 19), Roger Sherman (June 1, July 17), John Rutledge (June 1, July 19, September 5), Charles Pinckney (June 2, July 17, July 25, August 24) of South Carolina, and (sometimes) George Mason (July 25, 26). These delegates, along with many others, also voted in favor of this procedure on several occasions.[43]

Additionally, William Houstoun of Georgia moved, on July 24, that the executive be appointed by the national legislature instead of by electors appointed by the state legislatures (which had been approved on July 19). Madison reported that Houstoun "dwelt chiefly on the improbability, that capable men would undertake the service of Electors from the more distant States." Richard Dobbs Spaight of North Carolina seconded this motion, and Caleb Strong of Massachusetts argued in favor of it. The Convention granted the motion by a vote of seven ayes to four noes.[44]

A number of delegates objected to the selection of the executive by the national legislature. On June 2, Elbridge Gerry argued that this procedure would result in a constant intrigue kept up for the appointment. The legislature and the candidates would bargain and play into one another's hands. Votes would be given by the former under promises or expectations from the latter, of recompensing them by services to members of the legislature or to their friends.[45]

On June 9, Gerry again argued that appointment by the national legislature could lessen the national executive's independence and give birth to intrigue and corruption between the executive and the legislature before the election, as well as partiality in the executive afterward to the latter's supporters in the legislature.[46] According to New York delegate Robert Yates, Gerry "supposed that in the national legislature there will be a great number of bad men of various descriptions—these will make a wrong appointment. Besides, an executive thus appointed, will have his partiality in favor of those who appointed him ...."[47] On July 25, Gerry repeated his remark that an election of the executive by the national legislature "was radically and incurably wrong ...."[48]

On July 17, Gouverneur Morris "pointedly" opposed the election of the national executive by the national legislature, stating that the executive would then be a mere creature of the legislature. "If the Legislature elect, it will be the work of intrigue, of cabal, and of faction ... ; real merit will rarely be the title to the appointment."[49] Again, on July 24, Morris stated: "Of all possible modes of appointment [of the executive] that by the Legislature is the worst. If the Legislature is to appoint, and to impeach or to influence the impeachment, the Executive will be the mere creature of it. He had been opposed to the impeachment, but was now convinced that impeachments must be provided for, if the appt. was to be of any duration. **No man wd. say, that an Executive known to be in the pay of an Enemy, should not be removable in some way or other.**"[50]

On the same day, James Wilson said that an important objection against an absolute election of the executive by the legislature was that the executive in that case "would be too dependent to stand the mediator between the intrigues & sinister views of the Representatives and the general liberties & interests of the people."[51] He later repeated his opposition to the legislative appointment of the executive, concluding that it was notorious that this branch of business was the "most corruptly managed of any that had been committed to legislative bodies."[52]

"Certain it was," observed James Madison on July 19, "that the appointment [of the executive by the national legislature] would be attended by intrigues and contentions that ought not to be unnecessarily admitted." Madison delved deeply into political philosophy: "If it be a fundamental principle of free Govt. that the Legislative, Executive, & Judiciary powers should be *separately* exercised; it is equally so that they be *independently* exercised." A coalition of the legislative and executive powers "would be more immediately & certainly dangerous to public liberty" than a coalition of the legislative and judicial powers. "It is essential then that the appointment of the Executive should either be drawn from some source, or held by some tenure, that will give him a free agency with regard to the Legislature. This could not be if he was to be appointable from time to time by the Legislature."[53]

On July 25, Madison said that election of the executive by the national legislature "was in his Judgment liable to insuperable objections." He adduced three main reasons for this conclusion. First, such election "would agitate & divide the legislature so much that the public interest would materially suffer by it." Second, "the candidate would intrigue with the Legislature, would derive his appointment from the predominant faction, and be apt to render his administration subservient to its views. Third, "[t]he

Ministers of foreign powers would have and make use of, the opportunity to mix their intrigues & influence with the Election. Limited as the powers of the Executive are, it will be an object of great moment with the great rival powers of Europe who have American possessions, to have at the head of our Governmt. a man attached to their respective politics & interests. No pains, nor perhaps expence, will be spared, to gain from the Legislature an appointmt. favorable to their wishes."[54]

When, on July 26, the Convention voted to adopt a resolution for election of the executive by the national legislature, Madison made a point of stating in his notes that he and George Washington of the Virginia delegation voted against it. Two other members of the delegation, George Mason and John Blair, voted for the resolution. Since a fifth vote, Edmund Randolph, "happened to be out of the House," the delegation was tied and accordingly could not vote for or against the resolution. The resolution passed by a vote of six states to three with Massachusetts being absent.[55] If Randolph had been present, he undoubtedly would have voted aye, since he had consistently favored the election of the executive by the national legislature.

On July 25, South Carolina delegate Pierce Butler also opposed legislative election of the executive. "The two great evils to be avoided" he said, "are cabal at home, & influence from abroad. It will be difficult to avoid either if the Election be made by the national legislature."[56] At the same session, Hugh Williamson of North Carolina "was sensible that strong objections lay agst. an election of the Executive by the Legislature, and that it opened a door for foreign influence."[57] John Dickinson of Delaware agreed that "insuperable objections lay agst an election of the Executive by the Natl. Legislature . . . ."[58]

THE EVOLUTION OF THE ELECTORAL COLLEGE

The preceding sections of this chapter have disclosed the competing views of the Constitutional Convention delegates regarding proposals for direct popular election of the president and the election of the president by the national legislature. These discussions also revealed the first glimmerings of the concept of some kind of electoral college scheme. It is now time to learn how the Electoral College system that was eventually enshrined in the Constitution was formulated.

James Wilson of Pennsylvania strongly supported direct popular election of the national executive. On June 2, however, he proposed, as a compromise measure, that the national executive (president) be elected in the following manner: The states would be divided into districts, and the persons qualified to vote in each district for members of the first branch (House of Representatives) of the national legislature would elect members for their respective districts to be electors of the executive. The electors so chosen would meet at an agreed place and would proceed to elect by ballot someone outside of their

22

body "in whom the Executive authority of the national Government shall be vested."[59]

In arguing for this proposal, Wilson "repeated his arguments in favor of an election without the intervention of the States. He supposed too that this mode would produce more confidence among the people in the first magistrate, than an election by the national Legislature."[60]

Elbridge Gerry of Massachusetts professed to like the principle of Wilson's motion but feared "it would alarm & give a handle to the State partizans, as tending to supersede altogether the State authorities." Madison stated in his notes that Gerry "seemed to prefer the taking the suffrages of the States instead of Electors, or letting the [state] Legislatures nominate, and the electors appoint." But Gerry was "not clear that the people ought to act directly even in <the> choice of electors, being too little informed of personal characters in large districts and liable to deceptions."[61] Gerry's preferred method, in fact, was for the state governors to elect the national executive, a proposal that was defeated with no states voting in favor of it.[62] On July 19, he proposed that electors chosen by the state executives appoint the national executive, which apparently was not seconded and was not the subject of a vote.[63]

Hugh Williamson of North Carolina "could see no advantage" in Wilson's June 2 motion for popular election of presidential electors. Such electors chosen by the people would stand in the same relation to them as the state legislatures, "whilst the expedient would be attended with great trouble and expense."[64] In other words, since the people already elected state legislators, it would, in Williamson's view, just be a duplication of expense to have electors appointed. Though apparently not mentioned at the time, Williamson was ignoring the advantage of having electors appointed for one purpose and one purpose only, thereby not being subject to the normal twists and turns of legislative politics.

Wilson's motion for an electoral college elected by the people was rejected, with only two states (Pennsylvania and Maryland) voting for it.[65]

Immediately thereafter, eight states voted in favor of the Virginia Plan resolution to have the national executive appointed by the national legislature. Pennsylvania and Maryland voted against this proposition.[66]

On June 18, New York delegate Alexander Hamilton gave a long speech in which he advocated, among other things, the selection of a national executive by electors chosen by the people in district elections.[67] He evidently did not make a formal motion for this procedure, and no vote was held on it.

On July 7, Luther Martin of Maryland moved that the national executive be chosen by electors appointed by the state legislatures. Only Delaware and Maryland voted in favor of this proposal.[68]

As discussed earlier in this chapter, James Madison hinted on July 19 that the appointment of electors would "obviate" the "difficulty," as he put it, of the fact that southern slaves could not vote in a system of direct popular election of the executive, thereby weakening the political power of the southern states vis-à-vis the northern states. Although Madison's notes did not explain how electors would solve this alleged problem, he was very likely thinking that electors would be apportioned among the states according to their respective populations (as distinguished from the number of those admitted to the franchise), including three-fifths of a state's slaves. The Convention had adopted such a three-fifths formula for representation on July 12 and had additionally, on July 16, adopted the Great Compromise (also called the Connecticut Compromise) whereby the number of representatives in the first house of the national legislature (House of Representatives) would be apportioned to each state on the basis of that state's total population, including three-fifths of the slaves, but each state would have equal suffrage in the second house (Senate).[69]

On July 19, the Convention adopted the proposal of Connecticut delegate Oliver Ellsworth that the state legislatures should appoint electors to elect the national executive. The question of how the electors were to be apportioned among the states was postponed.[70] The following day, the Convention approved Elbridge Gerry's apportionment scheme whereby, for the first election of the national executive, New Hampshire, Rhode Island, Delaware, and Georgia would each have one elector; Connecticut, New York, New Jersey, Maryland, North Carolina, and South Carolina would each have two electors, and Massachusetts, Pennsylvania, and Virginia would each

25

have three electors.[71] Hugh Williamson proposed that in subsequent elections the electors be apportioned according to the number of representatives of each state in the first house (House of Representatives) of the national legislature. This motion, which was not seconded and not voted on at this time, was likely the kind of solution contemplated by Madison on July 19 when he said that the substitution of electors for direct popular vote would resolve the difficulty of the more diffusive northern suffrage.[72]

But all such calculations were soon rendered moot. On July 24 the Convention reversed its July 19 adoption of an electoral college scheme and voted instead to return to the concept of the executive being elected by the national legislature. A Committee of Detail was then appointed "to report a Constitution conformable to the Resolutions passed by the Convention."[73]

Madison and some other delegates refused, however, to accept the Convention's determination on July 24 that the national legislature should elect the executive. The next day, Madison gave an extended speech in which he analyzed the various possible modes of electing the executive. His attack on the use of the national legislature to elect the executive was discussed in the preceding section of this chapter. He also rejected the appointment of the national executive by the executives or legislatures of the state governments. State governors "could & would be courted, and intrigued with by the Candidates, by their partizans, and by the Ministers of foreign powers." State

26

legislatures, during the last several years, "had betrayed a strong propensity to a variety of pernicious measures."[74]

After dismissing appointments of the executive by the national legislature or by state executives or legislatures, Madison observed that "[t]he Option before us then lay between an appointment by Electors chosen by the people — and an immediate appointment by the people." He thought the appointment of electors by the people free from many of the objections that had been urged against it, and greatly preferable to an appointment by the national legislature. "As the electors would be chosen for the occasion, would meet at once, & proceed immediately to an appointment, there would be very little opportunity for cabal, or corruption. As a further precaution, it might be required that they should meet at some place, distinct from the seat of Govt. and even that no person within a certain distance of the place at the time shd. be eligible." Madison concluded, however, that this mode "had been rejected so recently & by so great a majority that it probably would not be proposed anew." Madison thus argued in favor of direct popular election of the national executive; those arguments are recounted in the first section of this chapter.[75]

But the majority of states in the Convention were still committed to the notion of election of the national executive by the national legislature. Delegates debated over and over again, day after day, week after week, month after month the issues of whether the executive would be corrupted by obtaining election from the legislature and, whether, in turn, the legislature would be corrupted by such a relationship with the executive. The possibility of foreign influence on sitting legislators was also repeatedly raised. Madison's point about separation of powers was difficult to refute. Dependence of the executive on election or reelection by the national legislature would make the office more like that of a prime minister in a parliamentary system than that of an independent president. Again and again, the delegates debated whether the executive should be limited to one term or, to the contrary, be eligible for a second term, the assumption being that the legislature would have more control over the executive if it had the power of reelection. Various schemes were advanced for mitigating such executive dependence on the legislature.[76]

On July 26, the Convention again voted in favor of election of the national executive by the national legislature. The executive's term would be seven years, with an ineligibility for a second term. Six states (New Hampshire, Connecticut, North Carolina, South Carolina, and Georgia) voted in favor of this resolution, three states (Pennsylvania, Delaware, and Maryland) voted against, and one state (Virginia) was divided (Madison and Washington voted against it). Massachusetts and New York were absent, and Rhode Island never attended the Convention.[77] This and other matters that had been determined by the Convention since the appointment of the Committee of Detail were referred to that committee. The Convention then adjourned until Monday, August 6, to give the Committee of Detail time, in Madison's words, "to prepare & report the Constitution."[78]

28

On August 6, the Committee of Detail submitted its report to the Convention. The report included a draft constitution that, among other things, provided for the election of what it called the "president" by the national legislature. The president would have a term of seven years and be ineligible for reelection.[79]

After discussions of other issues, the Convention addressed the method of selecting the president on August 24. The Committee of Detail had included the following language in its draft constitution: "The Executive Power of the U[nited] S[tates] shall be vested in a single person. His stile shall be 'The President of the U[nited] S[tates] of America;' . . . . He shall be elected by ballot by the Legislature. He shall hold his office during the term of seven years; but shall not be elected a second time."[80]

The proposed language that the president "shall be elected by ballot by the [national] Legislature" became the subject of fierce debate. John Rutledge of South Carolina moved to insert "joint" before the word "ballot." He considered this "the most convenient mode of electing."[81] Roger Sherman of Connecticut objected to a joint ballot "as depriving the *States* represented in the *Senate* of the negative intended them in that house."[82] The periodic battle between the large and small states was reignited.

During the debate about adding the word "joint" to the constitutional language, Daniel Carroll of Maryland suddenly moved to strike out "by the Legislature" and insert "by the people" so that the provision would read that the president "shall be elected by ballot by the people."

James Wilson of Pennsylvania seconded the motion. However, the motion failed, with nine states voting against it and only two states (Pennsylvania and Delaware) voting for it.[83]

In support of the motion to add "joint" to the word "ballot," James Madison made the following significant remarks: "If the amendment [for a joint ballot] be agreed to[,] the rule of voting will give to the largest State, compared with the smallest, an influence of 4 to 1 only, altho' the population is as 10 to 1. This surely cannot be unreasonable as the President is to act for the *people* not for the *States*."[84] This is one of many examples of Madison's strongly held conviction that the new constitution should be understood as created by the people. In contrast, William Paterson and some other small-state advocates argued that the emerging constitution should not depart from the plan of the Articles of Confederation, in which the central government was merely a league among states, each of which having but one vote in a unicameral legislature.[85]

After extended debate, the Convention voted in favor of inserting "joint" before "ballot," thereby amending the provision to read that the president "shall be elected by joint ballot by the [national] Legislature." Seven states voted aye; four voted no.[86]

With an additional amendment that day, the provision read: "He [the president] shall be elected by joint ballot by the Legislature, to which election a majority of the votes of the members present shall be required. He shall hold his office during the term of seven years; but shall not be elected a second time."[87]

After these developments, Gouverneur Morris of Pennsylvania rose to again express his opposition to the election of the president by the national legislature. He moved that the president "shall be chosen by Electors to be chosen by the people of the several States." Daniel Carroll of Maryland seconded the motion, but it was defeated with five ayes (Connecticut, New Jersey, Pennsylvania, Delaware, and Virginia) to six noes (New Hampshire, Massachusetts, Maryland, North Carolina, South Carolina, and Georgia).[88]

After a brief discussion of related matters, the Convention considered the first part (the president "shall be chosen by electors") of Gouverneur Morris's previous motion "as an abstract question" (Madison's words), but that proposition was defeated four states to four states with one state (Massachusetts) absent and two states (Connecticut and Maryland) equally divided.[89]

The progression of the votes on an electoral college concept was interesting. The states appeared to be moving to something like an even split as to whether some sort of electoral college scheme should be adopted. A bare majority of states, however, still did not approve of an electoral college chosen by the people.

A Committee of Eleven (one delegate from each state) was appointed on August 31 to consider "such parts of the Constitution as have been postponed, and such parts of Reports as have not been acted on . . . ." James Madison was appointed to this committee for Virginia. The other members of the committee were Nicholas Gilman (New Hampshire), Rufus King (Massachusetts), Roger Sherman (Connecticut), David Brearly (New Jersey), Gouverneur Morris (Pennsylvania), John Dickinson (Delaware), Daniel Carroll (Maryland), Hugh Williamson (North Carolina), Pierce Butler (South Carolina), and Abraham Baldwin (Georgia).[90] This committee is sometimes called the Committee on Postponed Parts.

The Committee of Eleven reported to the Convention on September 4. The report recommended the following new constitutional language regarding the election of the president:

> **He [the President] shall hold his office during the term of four years, and together with the Vice President, chosen for the same term, be elected in the following manner.**

> **Each State shall appoint in such manner as it's [*sic*] Legislature may direct, a number of Electors equal to the whole number of Senators, and Members of the House of Representatives to which the State may be entitled in the [national] legislature.**

> **The Electors shall meet in their respective States, and vote by ballot for two Persons, of whom one at least shall not be an inhabitant of the same State with themselves. — and shall make a list of all the Persons voted for,**

and of the number of votes for each, which list they shall sign and certify, and transmit sealed to the seat of the general Government, directed to the President of the Senate.

The President of the Senate shall in that House open all the certificates, and the votes shall be then and there counted — The Person having the greatest number of votes shall be the President, if such number be a majority of the Electors and if there be more than One, who have such Majority, and have an equal number of votes, then the Senate shall choose by ballot one of them for President: but if no Person have a majority, then from the five highest on the list, the Senate shall choose by ballot one of them for President — and in every case after the choice of the President, the Person having the greatest number of votes shall be Vice President: but if there should remain two or more, who have equal votes, the Senate shall choose from them the Vice President.

The [national] Legislature may determine the time of choosing and assembling the Electors, and the manner of certifying and transmitting their votes.[91]

The first three paragraphs quoted and emphasized above were incorporated into the final Constitution, with only a few stylistic changes. The emphasized portion of the fourth paragraph was similarly incorporated except that the final Constitution provided that the president of the Senate shall open all the certificates in the presence of **both** the Senate and the House of Representatives.

Thus, between the appointment of the Committee of Eleven on August 31 and the Committee's report on September 4, a fundamental change was effected in the method of selecting the president. For months, the Convention had always fallen back on the appointment of the president by the national legislature. Now, a committee, consisting of one member from each of the attending eleven states, recommended what became, with some later modifications by the Twelfth Amendment, the institution we know today as the Electoral College.

Although we do not have any records of this Committee of Eleven, John Dickinson, one of its members, explained in an 1802 letter how the Committee changed the procedure for appointing the president. It is worth quoting his account in full:

> One Morning the Committee met in the Library Room of the State House, and went upon the Business. I was much indisposed during the whole Time of the Convention. I did not come into the Committee till late, and found the members upon their Feet. **When I came in, they were pleased to read to Me their Minutes, containing a Report to this purpose, if I remember rightly—that the President**

should be chosen by the Legislature. The particulars I forget. I observed, that the Powers which we had agreed to vest in the President, were so many and so great, that I did not think, the people would be willing to deposit them with him, unless they themselves would be more immediately concerned in his Election—that from what had passed in Convention respecting the Magnitude and accumulation of those powers, We might easily judge what Impressions might be made on the Public Mind, unfavorable to the Constitution We were framing—that if this single Article should be rejected, the whole would be lost, and the States would have to work to go over again under vast Disadvantages—that the only true and safe Principle on which these powers could be committed to an Individual, was—that he should be in a strict sense of the Expression, *the Man of the People*—besides, that an Election by the Legislature, would form an improper Dependence and Connection. Having thus expressed my sentiments, Gouverneur Morris immediately said—"Come, Gentlemen, let us sit down again, and converse further on this subject." **We then all sat down, and after some conference, James Maddison took a Pen and Paper, and sketched out a Mode for Electing the President agreeable to the present provision. To this we assented and**

reported accordingly. These two Gentlemen, I dare say, recollect these Circumstances.[92]

Dickinson expressed a strong belief in this letter that the people, not the state legislatures, should choose the presidential electors. As we shall see in Chapters 3 and 4, this was not the way many state legislature interpreted the constitutional provision (Article II, Section 1, Clause 2) that "[e]ach State shall appoint, **in such Manner as the Legislature thereof may direct**, a Number of Electors equal to the whole number of Senators and Representatives to which the State may be entitled in the Congress; . . . ." (Emphasis added.)

The Committee's proposed text (quoted above) provided that the electors were to vote by ballot for two persons, without distinguishing between who should be president and who should be vice president. The arithmetic made it possible for more than one person to end up with the same number of majority votes for president. In that event, the Senate (changed a few days later to the House of Representatives, voting by states) was to choose by ballot one of the candidates tied for president. In the event no one received a majority of the electoral votes, the Senate (later the House) would decide who would be president from the top five candidates in the electoral vote. In all cases, the person having the greatest number of votes after the president would be vice president. If, however, two or more of the remaining candidates had an equal number of electoral votes, then the Senate would choose from among them who would be vice president.

A scenario in which the Electoral College fails to identify one person having a majority of votes for president, resulting in the election devolving on a legislative body, is called a "contingent election" in the Electoral College literature. The contingent election procedure of the Committee's report remained in the final Constitution except that the House of Representatives, voting by states, was substituted for the Senate in the case of presidential elections. The Senate still selected the vice president when the electoral vote failed to select a clear winner for that position. Much of the debate in the Convention on September 4, 5, and 6 concerned the procedures for such contingent elections.[93]

On September 6, the Convention voted to approve the following language of the Committee report by nine ayes to two nays (North Carolina and South Carolina): "Each State shall appoint in such manner as it's [*sic*] Legislature may direct, a number of Electors equal to the whole number of Senators, and Members of the House of Representatives to which the State may be entitled in the [national] legislature."[94]

On September 8, a Committee of Style was appointed to polish up the text of the entire Constitution in final form, and, on September 15, the Convention voted to approve the text of the Committee of Style, which made only a couple of stylistic improvements to the language quoted in the preceding paragraph. On September 17, the Constitution was signed by all delegates present, except for Edmund Randolph, George Mason, and Elbridge Gerry, who declined giving it the sanction of their names. The Convention then concluded its proceedings.[95]

FINAL TEXT OF THE 1787 CONSTITUTION REGARDING THE SELECTION OF THE PRESIDENT AND VICE PRESIDENT

The final text of the provisions on selection of the president and vice president in the 1787 Constitution, as submitted to the state conventions for ratification, was as follows:

Article II

Section 1

1. The executive Power shall be vested in a President of the United States of America. He shall hold his Office during the Term of four Years, and, together with the Vice President, chosen for the same Term, be elected, as follows:

2. Each State shall appoint, in such Manner as the Legislature thereof may direct, a Number of Electors, equal to the whole Number of Senators and Representatives to which the State may be entitled in the Congress: but no Senator or Representative, or Person holding an Office of Trust or Profit under the United States, shall be appointed an Elector.

3. The Electors shall meet in their respective States, and vote by Ballot for two Persons, of whom one at least shall not be an Inhabitant of the same State with themselves. And they shall make a List of all the Persons voted for, and of the Number of Votes for each; which List they shall sign and certify, and transmit sealed to the Seat of the Government of the United States, directed to the President of the Senate. The President of the Senate shall, in the Presence of the Senate and House of Representatives, open all the Certificates, and the Votes shall then be counted. The Person having the greatest Number of Votes shall be the President, if such Number be a Majority of the whole Number of Electors appointed; and if there be more than one who have such Majority, and have an equal Number of Votes, then the House of Representatives shall immediately chuse by Ballot one of them for President; and if no Person have a Majority, then from the five highest on the List the said House shall in like Manner chuse the President. But in chusing the President, the Votes shall be taken by States, the Representation from each State having one Vote; A quorum for this Purpose shall consist of a Member or Members from two thirds of the States, and a Majority of all the States shall be necessary to a Choice. In every Case, after

the Choice of the President, the Person having the greatest Number of Votes of the Electors shall be the Vice President. But if there should remain two or more who have equal Votes, the Senate shall chuse from them by Ballot the Vice President.

4. The Congress may determine the Time of chusing the Electors, and the Day on which they shall give their Votes; which Day shall be the same throughout the United States.[96]

The entire 1787 Constitution (including these provisions) was ratified by the requisite number of states on June 21, 1788. The first and second clauses (paragraphs) quoted above remain in effect as of the time of this writing. The entirety of the third clause set forth above was superseded by the Twelfth Amendment (ratified June 15, 1804).

JAMES MADISON'S LATER RECOLLECTION

Thirty-six years after the Convention, James Madison, in a letter to George Hay, wrote the following:

> The difficulty of finding an unexceptionable process for appointing the Executive Organ of a Govt. such as that of the U.S. was deeply felt by the Convention; and as the final arrangement of it took place in the latter stage of the Session, it was not exempt from a degree of the hurrying influence produced by fatigue

& impatience in all such bodies; tho' the degree was much less than usually prevails in them.

The part of the arrangement which casts the eventual appointment on the [House of Representatives] voting by States, was, as you presume, an accommodation to the anxiety of the smaller States for their sovereign equality, and to the jealousy of the larger States towards the cumulative functions of the Senate. The agency of the [House of Representatives] was thought safer also than that of the Senate, on account of the greater number of its members. It might indeed happen that the event would turn on one or two States having one or two [Representatives] only; but even in that case, the Representations of most of the States being numerous, the House would present greater obstacles to corruption, than the Senate with its paucity of Members.[97]

THE INTENTIONS OF THE FRAMERS OF THE ELECTORAL COLLEGE

What, then, were the intentions of the framers with regard to the provisions of the Constitution that provided for the selection of the president? As we have seen, the members of the 1787 Constitutional Convention had a variety of views. Most delegates eventually coalesced, however, on the text of Article II, Section 1 quoted above. The following conclusions can be derived from the facts set forth in the present chapter as well as from the contents of the more detailed Appendix. There were, of course, dissenters from these views, but the following represent the principles that eventually prevailed in the Convention and were incorporated into the final document.

First, the framers decisively rejected the lingering view that the president should be elected by the Congress and be dependent on it. The structure of Article II of the Constitution is that of an independent president in accordance with the principle of separation of powers. We do not have a parliamentary system in which a prime minister is elected by the legislature. The fear that an independent president would become a hereditary or elective monarch was addressed by the rules, including checks and balances, that the Constitution designed for the executive branch of government.

Second, the Constitution was a compromise between the view that the national government was solely an independent creature of the people and the view that the general government was purely a creation of the state governments. James Madison and his allies advocated the former of these propositions, and William Paterson and his allies represented the latter. Nationalists like Madison, James Wilson, and Gouverneur Morris were eventually forced, notwithstanding the impeccable logic of their arguments, to compromise with such advocates of state governmental power as William Paterson, Roger Sherman, and Oliver Ellsworth.[98] We see the results in a Senate in which states have equal suffrage and in which state legislatures (before the Seventeenth Amendment) chose the two senators allocated to each state. We also see the compromise reflected in the apportionment of presidential electors on the basis of the total of a state's senators (two) plus the number of its members of the House of Representatives; in a presidential electoral system in which the state legislatures were given the power to determine how their respective electors were to be appointed; and in a procedure for contingent elections in which the House of Representatives, with only one vote per state, chooses the president if the Electoral College fails to elect a majority president. None of these concessions was theoretically acceptable to Madison. Indeed, the remarkable length of the Convention's proceedings was largely a result of his and his allies' extended opposition to several of these demands. But the nationalists eventually compromised on the basis of the folk wisdom that that half a loaf is better than none.[99]

Third, the Electoral College was a compromise between the delegates who expressed support for direct popular vote (James Wilson, Gouverneur Morris, Daniel Carroll, Rufus King, James Madison, and John Dickinson) and those who felt that the people were too ignorant, uninformed, or susceptible to demagoguery to be trusted to elect a president directly (Elbridge Gerry, Roger Sherman, Charles Pinckney, George Mason, and perhaps Pierce Butler). Small-state advocates also feared that direct popular vote would result in the routine election of presidents from the large states. Another problem was the lack of a nominating procedure for a popular ballot. Since the delegates did not anticipate the rise of national political parties that would nominate presidential candidates, it seemed probable that direct popular vote would result in many candidates of whom none would receive a majority of the votes cast.

Fourth, the Electoral College was also a compromise between the states that had many slaves and those that had few or none. The southern states did not like direct popular vote, because their slaves did not vote. The final version of the Electoral College apportioned electors to each state on the basis of the total of the state's senators (two) and members of the House of Representatives. The number of a state's House members, in turn, was based on the state's total nonslave population (excepting Native Americans not taxed) plus three-fifths of its slaves. Thus, the widespread existence of slavery in the southern states gave them more electoral power vis-à-vis the northern states in the Electoral College than they would have had in a direct popular vote system.

Fifth, the strong and persistent movement in the Convention toward election of the president by the national legislature was ultimately defeated by the concerns about improper collusion between the president and Congress as well as foreign influence. In the final version of the Constitution, the electors were required to meet in their respective states, and the day on which they were to vote was "to be the same throughout the United States." Moreover, "no Senator or Representative, or Person holding an Office of Trust or Profit under the United States, shall be appointed an Elector." These provisions were considered to be insurance against corruption originating either at home or abroad. In fact, the term "Electoral College," which did not come into use until decades later, is something of a misnomer as applied to these constitutional provisions. The term suggests that the electors would meet at one place, deliberate there, and vote. This indeed was the assumption underlying some of the electoral college schemes considered earlier by the Convention. But that procedure was rejected in the interest of minimizing the possibility of either domestic or foreign corruption. Of course, as we shall see later, modern technology has made the possibility and, indeed, reality of subjecting the electors to domestic or foreign lobbying much more widespread than the framers would have thought possible.

Sixth, many of the delegates, from several different perspectives, wished to devise a system that would result in the election of the most qualified and ethical candidate for president. Again and again, in many different contexts, they articulated this objective. They thought, all things considered, that the Electoral College system would advance that goal better than the alternatives.

This chapter has focused on the intentions of the framers of the Electoral College procedures in the 1787 Constitution. We turn now to the understandings of the ratifiers.

Chapter 2: The Understandings of the Ratifiers of the Electoral College

James Madison's Approach to Constitutional Interpretation

Article VII of the Constitution provides: "The Ratification of the **Conventions** of nine States, shall be sufficient for the Establishment of this Constitution between the States so ratifying the Same." (Emphasis added.) On September 17, 1787, the Constitutional Convention resolved that the proposed Constitution be laid before the Confederation Congress, "and that it is the Opinion of this Convention, that it should afterwards be submitted to a **convention of Delegates, chosen in each State by the People thereof**, under the Recommendation of its Legislature, for their Assent and Ratification . . . ."[1] In submitting the report (including the proposed Constitution) of the Constitutional Convention to the states for ratification, the Confederation Congress "*Resolved* Unanimously that the said Report with the resolutions and letter accompanying the same be transmitted to a **convention of Delegates chosen in each state by the people thereof** in conformity to the resolves of the Convention made and provided in that case."[2]

The premise of the Constitution is that it would be ratified not by the state legislatures but by special conventions whose members were separately elected by the people of each state. This was one of Madison's most important contributions to the Constitution.[3]   As he remarked on August 31, "The people were in fact, the fountain of all power, and by resorting to them, all difficulties were got over. They could alter constitutions as they pleased."[4]

Madison placed great importance on the ratification of the Constitution by state conventions elected by the people. Americans at this time knew little about what had occurred in the Constitutional Convention.   They knew only its product: the proposed Constitution.   The proceedings themselves were conducted in secret.   Madison's notes constituted the only detailed account of the Convention, but Madison decided not to publish his notes of the Convention during his lifetime.   Although he died in 1836, his notes were not published until 1840—more than fifty years after the Convention.[5]

After the Constitution went into effect, Madison and Jefferson became involved in bitter disputes with Secretary of the Treasury Alexander Hamilton about the meaning of this document.   Although Madison himself had sometimes referred to discussions in the Constitutional Convention in arguing for a particular constitutional interpretation, his final position seemed to be that only the ratification debates were relevant.[6]   In an April 6, 1796 speech in the House of Representatives, Madison admitted that he had earlier cited his own recollection of the Convention proceedings, but now his view seemed to have changed:

But, after all, whatever veneration might be entertained for the body of men who formed our constitution, the sense of that body could never be regarded as the oracular guide in the expounding the constitution. As the instrument came from them, it was nothing more than the draught of a plan, nothing but a dead letter, until life and validity were breathed into it, by the voice of the people, speaking through the several state conventions. If we were to look therefore, for the meaning of the instrument, beyond the face of the instrument, we must look for it not in the general convention, which proposed, but in the state conventions, which accepted and ratified the constitution.[7]

He still held the same view more than three decades later: "Another error has been in ascribing to the *intention* of the *Convention* which formed the Constitution an undue ascendancy in expounding it. Apart from the difficulty of verifying that intention it is clear, that if the meaning of the Constitution is to [be] sought out[side] of itself, it is not in the proceedings of the Body that proposed it, but in those of the State Conventions which gave it all the validity and authority it possesses."[8] Nevertheless, it is quite possible that a reason Madison preferred the debates in the state ratifying conventions to his own unpublished record of the Constitutional Convention as a source of constitutional interpretation was that he had changed his mind about some important principles after the new government went into effect.[9] This may also explain his decision to disallow publication of his Constitutional Convention notes until after his death.[10]

In his April 6, 1796 speech, Madison noted that "[i]n referring to the debates of the state conventions as published, he wished not to be understood as putting entire confidence in the accuracy of them. Even those of Virginia, which had probably been taken down by the most skilful hand (whose merit he wished by no means to disparage) contained internal evidence in abundance of chasms [omissions], and misconceptions of what was said."[11] Indeed, as Professor Mary Sarah Bilder has observed, "Madison knew the paltry extent of these records."[12]

Madison also suggested that the "amendments proposed by the several conventions, were better authority and would be found on a general view to favour the sense of the constitution which had prevailed in this house [the House of Representatives in 1796]."[13] This notion appeared to be related to the specific subject at hand, which involved documents requested of President Washington by the House of Representatives relating to the Jay Treaty. In any event, it was an uncharacteristically weak argument of a type that is not accepted in constitutional or statutory interpretation.[14]

In a letter dated June 21, 1789, Madison discussed the difficulties that the first Congress was experiencing in establishing the new government. "Among other difficulties," he said, "the exposition of the Constitution is frequently a copious source, and must continue so until its meaning on all great points shall have been settled by precedents."[15] Madison had earlier made a similar point in *Federalist* No. 37: "All new laws, though penned with the greatest technical skill, and passed on the fullest and most mature deliberation, are considered as more or less obscure and equivocal, until their meaning be liquidated and ascertained by a series of particular discussions and adjudications."[16] This view appears to be yet another layer in Madison's complex understanding of proper constitutional interpretation.

Considering Madison's general view that the ratification debates might provide guidance in constitutional interpretation, let us examine those debates with regard to the question of the selection of the president by the Electoral College.

THE DISCUSSIONS IN THE RATIFICATION CONVENTIONS REGARDING THE ELECTORAL COLLEGE

In thinking about the ratification proceedings, historians and constitutional law scholars often use the term "understanding" rather than "intention" to refer to the frame of mind of the delegates to the respective state ratifying conventions and the people who elected them. After all, these individuals had a binary choice: either accept or reject the proposed Constitution. Moreover, "it is not immediately apparent how the historian goes about divining the true intentions or understandings of the roughly two thousand actors who served in the various conventions that framed and ratified the Constitution, much less the larger electorate that they claimed to represent."[17]

Fortunately, since this book will ultimately propose a constitutional amendment, we are not called upon to interpret a specific constitutional provision for the purpose of understanding how it should be applied today. We do not need to take a side in the loud debate over originalism. Rather, our immediate purpose is to learn how the framers and ratifiers thought about the Electoral College, as evidenced by their written and spoken words. The Electoral College provisions in the 1787 Constitution and in the later Twelfth Amendment are not ambiguous. The only question is whether the reasons for the Electoral College given by the framers and ratifiers retain an importance for our own time so as to preclude an attempt to amend those constitutional provisions.

The remainder of this section addresses instances in which delegates to state conventions made substantive remarks relevant to the issue of selection of the president in the Constitution. Several ratifying conventions are not included because no such relevant discussions can be found in the extant records.

Pennsylvania Convention

The Pennsylvania convention on ratification of the Constitution began on November 21 and ended December 15, 1787. Evidently, no delegate other than James Wilson, a member of the 1787 Constitutional Convention and a strong supporter of its proposed Constitution, addressed the provisions of Article II, Section 1 regarding the selection of the president.

On December 11, 1787, Wilson observed in the state convention that the "manner of appointing the President of the United States I find is not objected to, therefore I shall say little on that point." He noted, however, that the Constitutional Convention was "perplexed with no part of this plan so much as with the mode of choosing the President of the United States. For my own part, I think the most unexceptionable mode, next after the one prescribed in this Constitution, would be that practiced by the Eastern [northern] States and the State of New York . . . ." As discussed in the preceding chapter, those states elected their governors by direct popular vote. Wilson was being coy when he suggested that direct popular vote was his second-favorite system. We know from the preceding chapter that direct popular vote was, in fact, Wilson's preferred method, with an electoral college concept his second choice. And the electoral college procedure he initially supported as an alternative to direct popular vote did not involve the state governments; instead, he had proposed the popular election of the electors, not leaving it to state legislatures to determine how the electors would be appointed as did the final constitutional provision. He now observed in the Pennsylvania ratifying convention that the great majority of the Constitutional Convention delegates felt that direct popular vote of the president was impracticable, given the large extent of the country, and he stated further, without explanation, that "other embarrassments presented themselves."[18]

Wilson compared the Electoral College procedure in the Constitution with the chief alternative discussed at the Constitutional Convention: appointment of the president by the national legislature with ineligibility for a second term. He stated that the latter method would violate the principle of separation of powers between the legislature and the executive, and "still stronger objections could be urged against that—cabal, intrigue, corruption—everything bad would have been the necessary concomitant of every election."[19]

In contrast, he added, the Electoral College procedures of the Constitution would bring the choice of the president "as nearly home to the people as is practicable; with the approbation of the state legislatures, the people may elect with only one remove," citing the provision in Article II, Section 1, Clause 2 of the Constitution that each state shall appoint its allocation of electors in such manner as the legislature thereof may direct. The Constitution, by requiring that the day on which the electors shall give their votes shall be the same throughout the United States, would make it difficult to corrupt the electors, "and there will be little time or opportunity for tumult or intrigue." Referring to the historical episodes that the framers often cited as the poster child of foreign influence, Wilson concluded: "This, Sir, will not be like the elections of a Polish diet, begun in noise and ending in bloodshed."[20]

Massachusetts Convention

There was little discussion in the Massachusetts ratifying convention of the procedures for electing the president. On January 28, 1788, Nathaniel Gorham, who had also been a delegate to the 1787 Constitutional Convention, observed that the Electoral College procedure was chosen because the people at large could not choose the president and because the Congress could not choose the president without the president becoming their creature. The available records do not state whether or how Gorham elaborated on these points.[21]

On the same day, Gorham stated that the reason why each presidential elector was required to cast two undifferentiated votes was that the small-states delegates said that if only one vote per elector were cast, a president would never be selected from a small state.[22] However, this procedure was later changed by the Twelfth Amendment, discussed in Chapter 3.

On February 6, Rev. Samuel Stillman observed that the "President and Senators are to be chosen by the interposition of the legislatures of the several States; who are the representatives and guardians of the people; whose honour and interest will lead them, in all human probability, to have good men placed in the general government."[23] As we saw in Chapter 1, this Pollyannaish view of the state legislatures was not shared by such nationalists as James Madison, James Wilson, and Alexander Hamilton, all of whom were both framers of the

Constitution in the 1787 Constitutional Convention and delegates to their respective state ratifying conventions.

Maryland Convention

Samuel Chase was one of the delegates to the Maryland ratifying convention. At this time Chase was an Antifederalist opponent of the Constitution. He delivered a lengthy speech in the convention on April 24 and 25, 1788. Although no transcript of the proceedings exists, Chase prepared a long list of objections to the Constitution, which he very probably addressed in his speech. Among many other things, **he objected to the Constitution "[b]ecause the *president* will not be chosen by the people *immediately*"; the state legislatures "are to direct *who are to be* electors . . . ."**[24]

Chase's political views later changed, and President George Washington appointed him to the U.S. Supreme Court. In those years, Supreme Court justices were obligated to be judges in some trial courts. After Thomas Jefferson became president, Chase was impeached by the House of Representatives for his inflammatory political remarks made while he was a sitting judge in trial court proceedings. He was, however, acquitted by the Senate.

Because the Maryland convention only lasted a few days and no one took stenographic notes or even summarized the proceedings, we do not know whether other relevant remarks were made by the delegates.

Virginia Convention

The Virginia ratifying convention was well documented, and several major political figures were delegates to it. Patrick Henry, George Mason, James Monroe, and William Grayson were Antifederalist opponents of the ratification of the Constitution. Those supporting the Constitution included James Madison, Governor Edmund Randolph (who had come around to supporting the Constitution after refusing to sign it at the Constitutional Convention), Judge Edmund Pendleton, and John Marshall, who later became chief justice of the U.S. Supreme Court.[25] Monroe and Grayson evidently wrote out their main speeches at the Virginia convention and gave the writings to the stenographic reporter, thereby ensuring a greater degree of accuracy in the reports of their speeches than the speeches of delegates who did not utilize such procedure. The reporter had difficulty hearing the soft-spoken Madison and also had significant problems transcribing Henry's speeches.[26]

On June 10, 1788, Governor Randolph stated: "How is the President elected? By the people—on the same day throughout the United States—by those whom the people please. There can be no concert between the electors. The votes are sent sealed to Congress."[27] Randolph's statement was somewhat misleading. The Constitution authorized the state legislatures to determine how their respective electors were to be chosen. In actual elections conducted after the ratification of the Constitution, several state legislatures themselves appointed the electors without holding a popular election.[28] Randolph was correct, however, in observing that the constitutional procedures regarding electors minimized the possibility of collusion.

On June 17, George Mason, an Antifederalist, attacked the Constitution on the ground that it did not require rotation in office of the president. The concept of rotation in office was essentially a term limit but often with an ability of the officer to return to the office at a later date. For example, Article V of the Articles of Confederation required that "no person shall be capable of being a delegate for more than three years in any term of six years." Several states had similar requirements for their public officials.[29] Mason argued for rotation in office of the president on several occasions at the 1787 Constitutional Convention. Having been defeated there, he strenuously advanced his argument in the Virginia convention. Mason asserted that "[t]his President will be elected time after time. He will be continued in office for life. If we wish to change him, the great powers of Europe will not allow us."[30]

Mason continued: "Will not the great powers of Europe, as France and Great-Britain, be interested in having a friend in the President of the United States; and will they not be more interested in his election, than in that of the King of Poland?" Although the people of Poland had a right to displace their king, Mason argued, they never do, because Prussia, Russia, and other European powers would not allow it. Likewise, "[t]he powers of Europe will interpose [in the U.S. election], and we shall have a civil war in the bowels of our country, and be subject to all the horrors and calamities of an elective Monarchy." Under the Constitution, the president could, with the consent of Congress, "receive a stated pension from European Potentates. This is an idea not altogether new in America. It is not many years ago, since the revolution, that a foreign power offered emoluments to persons holding offices under our Government. It will moreover be difficult to know, whether he receives emoluments from foreign powers or not." Mason concluded his speech by alleging that the electors meeting in their separate states could be easily influenced and that the only solution was a regular rotation of office of the president.[31]

Antifederalists like Mason feared that a president would be repeatedly elected, thereby becoming, in effect, an elected king. However, the first president, George Washington, declined standing for office for a third term, and that informal precedent was followed until the presidency of Franklin D. Roosevelt in the twentieth century. In the election of 1940, Roosevelt decided to run for a third term in view of the growing menace from Nazi Germany. Roosevelt won that election. He also won the election of 1944, during World War II, for his fourth term. He died on April 12, 1945, during his fourth term, shortly before the unconditional surrender of Germany.

In order to prevent a president from serving more than two terms, Congress, at the instigation of Republican legislators, adopted a proposed constitutional amendment and sent it to the states, where it was duly ratified on February 27, 1951, becoming the Twenty-Second Amendment to the Constitution. This amendment provided that "[n]o person shall be elected to the office of the President more than twice, and no person who has held the office of President, or acted as President, for more than two years of a term to which some other person was elected President shall be elected to the office of President more than once." Accordingly, the scenario of a repeatedly elected president becoming, in effect, an elective monarch for life is no long constitutionally possible. In the long view of constitutional history, Mason eventually prevailed on this point.

On June 18, 1788, James Monroe, then an Antifederalist, attacked the provisions in the proposed Constitution regarding the election of the president. He argued that the president "ought to act under the strongest impulses of rewards and punishments, which, are the strongest incentives to human actions." There are, he added, two ways of securing this point. "He ought to depend on the people of America for his appointment and continuance in office: He ought also to be responsible in an equal degree to all the States; and to be tried by dispassionate Judges: His responsibility ought further to be direct and immediate." Monroe argued that the president was insufficiently dependent on the people of America: "**He is to be elected by Electors, in a manner perfectly dissatisfactory to my mind. I believe that he will owe**

his election, in fact, to the State Governments, and not to the people at large."[32]

After hypothesizing how Congress might manipulate the electors, Monroe addressed the problem of foreign influence:

> **The situation of the United States, as it applies to the European States, demands attention.** We may hold the balance among those States. Their Western territories are contiguous to us. What we may do without any offensive operations, may have considerable influence. Will they not then endeavor to influence [the president's] general councils? May we not suppose that they will endeavour to attach him to their interest, and support him, in order to make him serve their purposes? If this be the case, does not the mode of election present a favorable opportunity to continue in office the person that shall be President? **I am persuaded they may, by their power and intrigues, influence his re-election. There being nothing to prevent his corruption, but his virtue, which is but precarious, we have not sufficient security.**[33]

Monroe also criticized the office of the vice president as being unnecessary. Because the vice president is to succeed the president in case of removal, disability, and so forth, **this "will render foreign powers desirous of**

securing his favor, to obtain which they will exert themselves in his behalf." [34]

Monroe concluded his speech with the following remarks: **"The President might be elected by the people, dependent upon them, and responsible for mal-administration. As this is not the case, I must disapprove of this clause in its present form."** [35]

William Grayson reinforced Monroe's concern about the possibility of foreign influence on the president: "I think we have every thing to apprehend from such interferences. It is highly probable the President will be continued in office for life. To gain his favor they will support him. Consider the means of importance he will have by creating officers. If he has a good understanding with the Senate, they will join to prevent a discovery of his misdeeds." [36]

George Mason then again returned to the battle. He "contended that this mode of election was a mere deception—a mere *ignus fatuus* [delusive hope] on the people of America, and thrown out to make them believe they were to choose [the president]; whereas it would not be once out of fifty that he would be chosen by them in the first instance; because a majority of the whole number of [electoral] votes was required." Mason objected to the contingent election procedure of the House of Representatives voting by states. "The people will in reality have no hand in his election." [37]

James Madison then responded to the Antifederalist critics of the mode of selecting the president:

> The choice of the people ought to be attended to. I have found no better way of selecting the man in whom they place the highest confidence, than that delineated in the plan of the Convention— nor has the Gentleman [Mason] told us. **Perhaps it will be found impracticable to elect [the president] by the immediate suffrages of the people. Difficulties would arise from the extent and population of the States. Instead of this, the people choose the Electors.— This can be done with ease and convenience, and will render the choice more judicious.**[38]

As previously discussed, the notion that the people choose the electors under the Constitution is not correct. Rather, the Constitution authorizes each state legislature to determine how the electors for their state will be chosen, and many state legislatures in the early decades of the republic decided to choose their electors themselves without any involvement of the people.

Madison also expressed approval of the contingent election procedures stipulated in the original Article II, Section 1, Clause 3 of the Constitution. He said that the use of the House of Representatives, voting by states, was a compromise to placate the small states. The larger states would have an advantage in the election. If, however, a majority of electors did not vote for one candidate, the smaller states would have an advantage in the contingent election.[39]

After debate on other issues, Madison returned to the constitutional provisions regarding the mode of selection of the president on June 20: "It may be proper to remark, that the organization of the General Government for the United States [in the Constitutional Convention], was, in all its parts, very difficult. **There was a peculiar difficulty in that of the Executive. Every thing incident to it, must have participated of that difficulty. That mode which was judged most expedient was adopted, till experience should point out one more eligible.**"[40]

Madison's June 20 remark was a brief digression from his response to George Mason regarding the judicial powers in Article III. In the context of these proceedings, it was an addendum to Madison's remarks on June 18 regarding the mode of election of the president by the Electoral College.[41] (The June 19 session dealt with the treaty and judicial powers and did not address the mode of election of the president.[42]) On June 20, Madison, after further reflection, appeared to be attempting to assure his friend Monroe that a constitutional amendment might be appropriate in the event "experience should point out [a mode of election] more eligible" than the Electoral College procedure. As observed above, Monroe had opposed the Electoral College on June 18, arguing that the president should depend on the people and not on the states for election. Madison, who had indicated substantial sympathy in the Constitutional Convention for direct popular vote in presidential elections, appeared already to be contemplating a constitutional amendment to abolish the Electoral College in favor of popular election of the president.

North Carolina Convention

At the North Carolina ratifying convention, both William Richardson Davie, who was a delegate to the Constitutional Convention, and James Iredell, who was not, misspoke when they respectively said that the electors would be appointed by the people.[43] As discussed earlier, Article II, Section 1, Clause 2 of the Constitution provided, and still provides, that the electors are to be appointed "in such Manner as the [state] Legislature . . . may direct," and several state legislatures in the early decades of the republic chose to elect the presidential electors themselves instead of by a vote of the people. The North Carolina governor, Samuel Johnston, noted that some people thought that the state legislatures were to appoint the electors.[44]

Davie argued that the mode of election of the president "precludes every possibility of corruption or improper influence of any kind." Iredell agreed.[45]

On July 28, 1788, Iredell stated:

> It is of the greatest consequence to the happiness of the people of America, **that the person to whom this great trust [the presidency] is delegated should be worthy of it**. It would require **a man of abilities and experience**; it would also require a man who possessed, in a high degree, the confidence of his country. This

being the case, **it would be a great defect, in forming a constitution for the United States, if it was so constructed that, by any accident, an improper person could have a chance to obtain that office.**[46]

This North Carolina convention did not ratify the Constitution. On August 2, 1788, it voted to withhold ratification until such time as either Congress or a new general constitutional convention considered their proposed bill of rights and additional amendments. A second convention commenced on November 16, 1789, several months after the new general government began operations and a few weeks after Congress had approved constitutional amendments and sent them to the states for ratification. This second North Carolina convention then ratified the Constitution, leaving Rhode Island as the only state that had not ratified. Rhode Island finally ratified the Constitution on May 29, 1790.[47]

OTHER 1787-88 PUBLIC DISCUSSIONS REGARDING THE ELECTORAL COLLEGE

Many students of the ratification of the Constitution also try to glean the meaning of that document from the contemporaneous debates outside of the state ratification conventions. This makes some sense in that the people selected their delegates to the state constitutional conventions, and the popular understandings of the Constitution may be reflected in the wider discussion of whether or not it should be ratified. Accordingly, we shall look at what was said or written in these sources with regard to the selection of the president. As a result of the large quantity of written records of these public discussions, however, it is possible that the following account may miss some of the statements on this subject.

James Wilson's Speech in the State House Yard, Philadelphia, October 6, 1787

In this speech, Wilson addressed the accusation that the proposed Constitution was "not only calculated, but designedly framed, to reduce the state governments to mere corporations, and eventually to annihilate them." In response, Wilson first discussed the meaning of the word "corporation": "In common parlance, indeed, it is generally applied to petty associations for the ease and conveniency of a few individuals," but in its enlarged sense, the word comprehends the government of Pennsylvania, the existing union of states under the Articles of Confederation, and the projected government under the Constitution.[48]

Wilson then called attention to the manner in which the president, Senate, and House of Representatives were proposed to be appointed under the Constitution. "The President is to be chosen by Electors nominated in such manner as the legislature of each state may direct; so that if there is no legislature, there can be no Electors, and consequently the office of President cannot be supplied." Wilson then went on to discuss how the Senate and House of Representatives were to be chosen under the proposed

Constitution. The state legislatures selected each state's two senators (before the Seventeenth Amendment, ratified April 8, 1913). The House of Representatives is elected by those people who are qualified, by state statute, to vote for the most numerous branch of the state legislature. "From this view, then it is evidently absurd to suppose that the annihilation of the separate [state] governments will result from their union . . . ." In each case, absent the state governments, there can be no federal government.[49]

Wilson's early speech was widely printed, both in the Pennsylvania press and in newspapers all over the country. Other advocates of the Constitution repeated his arguments. In this way, according to an eminent historian, the speech "became a fundamental text for the ratification debates."[50]

Debate in the South Carolina House of Representatives, January 17-18, 1788

The South Carolina House of Representatives conducted a debate on the issue of ratification of the Constitution in January 1788. Although the later ratifying convention evidently did not address any issue about the selection of the president, some remarks about this topic were made in the House of Representatives debate.

On January 17, 1788, Rawlins Lowndes argued that it would be difficult for any one candidate to win a majority of the electoral votes, as was required by the proposed Constitution. Although George Washington would be the overwhelming favorite for the first election, Lowndes saw a problem in selecting a president after Washington. He doubted that any candidate would receive a majority of the electoral votes, "and if no gentleman should be returned, then this omnipotent government would be at a stand." Moreover, Lowndes predicted, a president would "never be looked for in this state—we should know nothing of him but by name."[51]

On January 18, Gen. Charles Cotesworth Pinckney, who had been a delegate to the 1787 Constitutional Convention, queried what other mode of electing the president would have been more proper than that of the proposed Constitution. Election by both the national House of Representatives and Senate as well as election by either of them would have diminished the independence of the president. But **"as he is to be elected by the people, through the medium of electors chosen particularly for that purpose,** and he is in some measure to be a check on the senate and the house of representatives, the election, in my opinion, could not have been placed so well if it had been made in any other mode." Foreign influence is to be guarded against in all elections of a chief magistrate. "[H]ere it is carefully so, as **it is almost impossible for any foreign power to influence thirteen different sets of electors, distributed throughout the states, from New-Hampshire to Georgia . . . ."** Similarly, **"the dangers of intrigue and corruption are avoided, and a variety of other inconveniencies which must have arisen if the electors from the different states had been directed to assemble in one place, or if either branch of the legislature (in case the majority of electors did not fix** upon the same person) might have chosen a president who had not been previously put into nomination by the people."[52]

Antifederalist Arguments in the Press

According to the editors of The Documentary History of the Ratification of the Constitution, "The best Antifederalist writing on the Constitution was a forty-page pamphlet entitled Observations Leading to a Fair Examination of the System of Government Proposed by the Late Convention; and to Several Essential and Necessary Alterations in It. In a Number of Letters from the Federal Farmer to the Republican." This pamphlet, whose authorship is not definitively known, was distributed in several states and played an important role in the ratification debates. Letter III, dated October 10, 1787, stated: **"The election of [the vice president], as well as of the president of the United States seems to be properly secured"** in the proposed Constitution.[53] As will be discussed below, Alexander Hamilton referred to this admission in his Federalist No. 68.

In the December 6, 1787 issue of a Boston newspaper called the *Independent Chronicle*, "Candidus" (a pseudonym) criticized the Electoral College provisions of the proposed Constitution, by arguing that **"the choice of president by a detached body of electors was dangerous and tending to bribery . . . ."**[54]

"A Countryman" (New York Antifederalist De Witt Clinton) wrote in the December 13, 1787 issue of the *New*

York Journal that "very little dependence can be put on the president-general [*sic*], and the senate [appointed by the state legislatures in the original Constitution], that **they are to be appointed in a very odd manner, and would be so far above the common people, that they will care little about them, and when they get themselves fairly fixed in the saddle, there will be no such thing as to get them out again . . . ."**[55]

"A Columbian Patriot" (Massachusetts Antifederalist Mercy Warren) wrote in her February 1788 pamphlet *Observations on the New Constitution and on the Federal and State Conventions* that "[i]f the sovereignty of America is designed to be elective, **the circumscribing the votes to only ten electors in this State [Massachusetts], and the same proportion in all the others, is nearly tantamount to the exclusion of the voice of the people in the choice of their first magistrate. It is vesting the choice solely in an aristocratic junto, who may easily combine in each State to place at the head of the Union the most convenient instrument for despotic sway."**[56]

The Federalist

During the ratification process in 1787 and 1788, three eminent personages—Alexander Hamilton, John Jay, and James Madison—wrote eighty-five essays supporting the proposed Constitution under the collective pseudonym "Publius." These were published, first, as separate newspaper articles. Later, they were combined in various editions collectively called *The Federalist*. These papers remain one of the principal documents consulted by scholars in attempting to understand the meaning of the provisions of the Constitution.

Hamilton and/or Jay, both residents of the state of New York, conceived of this project after reading several attacks on the proposed Constitution in the New York press. *The Federalist* essays were originally designed for New York audiences. Although some of them were published in other states, it was not until late May of 1788, after several states had already conducted their ratification conventions, that both volumes of the compiled essays were available.[57] But the Virginia convention, at which Madison was a delegate, did not commence until June 2, and the New York convention, at which both Hamilton and Jay were delegates, did not meet until June 17. The North Carolina convention did not start until July 21, and the Rhode Island convention was conducted after the new government went into effect.[58]

The mode of appointment of the president is the subject of *Federalist* No. 68, authored by Hamilton and first appearing on March 12, 1788. It begins with the observation that this constitutional provision "is almost the only part of the system, of any consequence, which has escaped without severe censure, or which has received the slightest mark of approbation from its opponents. The most plausible of these, who has appeared in print, has even deigned to admit, that the election of the president is pretty well guarded." Hamilton cited *The Federal Farmer* for this proposition.[59] Indeed, as noted earlier in this chapter, *The Federal Farmer*, an Antifederalist tract, did admit that the election of the president and vice president "seems to be properly secured."[60] However, the preceding subsection of this book cites examples of Antifederalist objections to the Constitution's method of selecting the president before *Federalist* No. 68 was published. And, as discussed earlier in the present section, Rawlins Lowndes had substantial doubts about these procedures on January 17 in the South Carolina House of Representatives. We have also seen criticisms of the electoral system after the publication of *Federalist* No. 68 in the state ratifying conventions of Maryland and Virginia.

Hamilton's essay emphasized the importance of having a select intermediate body, which we now call the Electoral College, between the people and the ultimate election of the president. First, "the sense of the people should operate in the choice of the person to whom so important a trust was to be confided. This end will be answered by committing the right of making it, not to any pre-established body, but to men, chosen by the people for the special purpose, and at the particular conjuncture."[61] Hamilton nowhere explicitly mentions in *Federalist* No. 68 that the constitutional provision states that each state legislature can decide for itself how its electors are chosen. He suggests that "the people" choose the electors, but he does not mention the fact, borne out in the history of the early decades of the republic, that the state legislatures themselves have the power to choose the electors without consulting the people.

73

Second, Hamilton thought it very important to have this select group of electors exercise their own judgment in electing a president:

> It was equally desirable, that **the immediate election should be made by men most capable of analizing [analyzing] the qualities adapted to the station**, and acting under circumstances favourable to deliberation and to a judicious combination of all the reasons and inducements, which were proper to govern their choice. **A small number of persons, selected by their fellow citizens from the general mass, will be most likely to possess the information and discernment requisite to so complicated an investigation.**[62]

Hamilton also stressed that it was "peculiarly desirable, to afford as little opportunity as possible to tumult and disorder." He emphasized the precautions that the Constitutional Convention had prescribed with regard to the electors:

> The choice of *several* to form an intermediate body of electors, will be much less apt to convulse the community, with any extraordinary or violent movements, than the choice of *one* who was himself to be the final object of the public wishes. And as the electors, chosen in each state, are to assemble and vote in the state, in which they are chosen, this detached

74

and divided situation will expose them much less to heats and ferments, which might be communicated from them to the people, than if they were all to be convened at one time, in one place.[63]

As detailed in Chapter 1, the delegates to the 1787 Constitutional Convention frequently discussed the need to avoid corruption, cabal, and intrigue, especially that instigated by foreign powers. Hamilton emphasized in *Federalist* No. 68 how the framers had guarded against such evils:

Nothing was more to be desired, than that **every practicable obstacle should be opposed to cabal, intrigue and corruption**. These most deadly adversaries of republican government might naturally have been expected to make their aproaches from more than one quarter, but **chiefly from the desire in foreign powers to gain an improper ascendant in our councils. How could they better gratify this, than by raising a creature of their own to the chief magistracy of the union?** But the convention have guarded against all danger of this sort with the most provident and judicious attention. They have not made the appointment of the president to depend on any pre-existing bodies of men who might be tampered with before hand to prostitute their votes; but they have referred it in the first instance to an immediate act of the people of America, to be exerted in the choice of persons for the temporary and sole purpose of making the appointment. And they have excluded from eligibility to this trust, all those who from situation might be suspected of too great devotion to the president in office. No senator, representative, or other person holding a place of trust or profit under the United States, can be of the number of the electors. Thus, without corrupting the body of the people, the immediate agents in the election will at least enter upon the task, free from any sinister byass [bias]. Their transient existence, and their detached situation, already taken notice of, afford a satisfactory prospect of their continuing so, to the conclusion of it. The business of corruption, when it is to embrace so considerable a number of men, requires time, as well as means. Nor would it be found easy suddenly to embark [engage] them, dispersed as they would be over thirteen states, in any combinations, founded upon motives, which though they could not properly be denominated corrupt, might yet be of a nature to mislead them from their duty.[64]

Hamilton also approved the contingent election procedure in the proposed Constitution, whereby the House of Representatives, voting by states, selected the president out of the candidates having the five highest numbers of

76

votes, in the event no one candidate received a majority of electoral votes that was higher than that of any other candidate.

Hamilton summed up his praise of the proposed electoral system as follows:

> This process of election affords a moral certainty, that **the office of president, will seldom fall to the lot of any man, who is not in an eminent degree endowed with the requisite qualifications**. Talents for low intrigue and the little arts of popularity may alone suffice to elevate a man to the first honors in a single state; but it will require other talents and a different kind of merit to establish him in the esteem and confidence of the whole union, or of so considerable a portion of it as would be necessary to make him a successful candidate for the distinguished office of president of the United States. **It will not be too strong to say, that there will be a constant probability of seeing the station filled by characters preeminent for ability and virtue.** And this will be thought no inconsiderable recommendation of the constitution, by those, who are able to estimate the share, which the executive in every government must necessarily have in its good or ill administration. . . . [W]e may safely pronounce, that **the true test of a**

good government is its aptitude and tendency to produce a good administration.[65]

Hamilton also made a reference in *Federalist* No. 77 to "the election of the president once in four years by persons immediately chosen by the people for that purpose."[66] Once again, we see Hamilton suggesting that the people immediately choose the electors, whereas the actual constitutional provision states that the electors of each state shall be appointed "in such Manner as the Legislature thereof may direct . . . ."[67]

Other *Federalist* essays also mentioned the mode of electing the president but did so in passing in various contexts.

Federalist No. 64 by John Jay addressed Article II, Section 2, Clause 2 of the proposed Constitution, which authorizes the president, by and with the advice and consent of the Senate, to make treaties. Jay emphasized the importance of this power being exercised by "men the best qualified for the purpose, and in the manner the most conducive to the public good." With specific reference to the president, Jay observed that the 1787 Constitutional Convention was attentive to these considerations by "direct[ing] the president to be chosen by select bodies of electors . . . ." Anticipating Hamilton's more extensive *Federalist* No. 68, Jay stated:

As the select assemblies for choosing the president . . . will, in general, be composed of

the most enlightened and respectable citizens, there is reason to presume, that their attention and their votes will be directed to **those men only who have become the most distinguished by their abilities and virtue**, and in whom the people perceive just grounds for confidence. . . . **[A]n assembly of select electors possess . . . the means of extensive and accurate information relative to men and characters**; so will their appointments bear . . . marks of discretion and discernment. The inference which naturally results from these considerations is this, that **the president . . .** so chosen, **will always be of the number of those who best understand our national interests, whether considered in relation to the several states or to foreign nations, who are best able to promote those interests, and whose reputation for integrity inspires and merits confidence.**[68]

Federalist Nos. 64 and 68 had essentially the same rationale. Both Jay and Hamilton thought that what we now call the Electoral College would be composed of wise individuals who would exercise their independent judgment and discretion in electing a president who possessed knowledge, wisdom, and integrity. They did not anticipate that electors would be selected on the basis of their fidelity to a particular political party and be expected to vote in accordance with the opinions of the majority of voters in their respective states.

James Madison touched on the Electoral College in *Federalist* Nos. 39 and 45 and perhaps indirectly in *Federalist* No. 10. In the latter essay, Madison distinguished between a pure democracy, in which "a small number of citizens . . . assemble and administer the government in person," and a republic, "in which the scheme of representation takes place . . . ." Madison wrote that the "two great points of difference between a democracy and a republic, are first, the delegation of the government, in the latter, to a small number of citizens elected by the rest; secondly, the greater number of citizens, and greater sphere of country, over which the latter may be extended." Madison argued that "[t]he effect of the first difference is, on the one hand, **to refine and enlarge the public views, by passing them through the medium of a chosen body of citizens, whose wisdom may best discern the true interest of their country, and whose patriotism and love of justice, will be least likely to sacrifice it to temporary or partial considerations.**"[69] Madison was specifically referring to the concept of representation, but his reasoning here has also been cited in the context of the Electoral College.[70] To the extent, if any, that Madison was thinking of the Electoral College, his statement is similar to those of Jay in *Federalist* No. 64 and Hamilton in *Federalist* No. 68.

Finally, Madison and other supporters of the proposed Constitution were faced with severe Antifederalist critiques that their ultimate purpose was to destroy the state governments. Madison responded in *Federalist* No. 39 that each branch of the proposed federal government depended on the state governments for its existence. For example, "[t]he immediate election of the president is to be made by the states in their political characters. The votes allotted to them, are in a compound ratio, which considers them partly as distinct and co-equal societies; partly as unequal members of the same society." Madison was referring here to the apportionment of electors to a state based on the number of the state's senators (two per state) plus the number of the state's representatives in the House of Representatives (the number per state varied, depending on population, with each slave being counted as three-fifths of a person). Similarly, in the event no candidate wins a majority of electoral votes that is also more electoral votes than any other candidate, the contingent election is with the House of Representatives, voting by states (one vote per state).[71] In *Federalist* No. 45, Madison wrote: "Without the intervention of the state legislatures, the president of the United States cannot be elected at all. They must in all cases have a great share in his appointment, and will perhaps in most cases of themselves determine it."[72] Madison here more accurately represented the constitutional language in Article II, Section 1, Clause 2 than did his colleague Hamilton, though, as we have seen, he incorrectly argued in the Virginia convention that "the people choose the Electors."

THE UNDERSTANDINGS OF THE RATIFIERS OF THE ELECTORAL COLLEGE

What, then, can we say about the understandings of the ratifiers of the Constitution, who, in ratifying that instrument, necessarily ratified its Electoral College provisions? A review of the present chapter suggests the following conclusions.

First, some Antifederalists objected to the Electoral College procedure whereby the people could not vote directly for the president and vice president. In response to such criticisms from his friend James Monroe, among others, James Madison indicated in the Virginia ratifying convention that a future amendment of this constitutional provision would be appropriate if experience proved another mode of election to be "more eligible."

Second, both supporters and opponents of the proposed Constitution stressed the need to avert "cabal, intrigue, and corruption" (in Hamilton's words), especially the danger of foreign influence.

Third, some of the advocates of the proposed Constitution inaccurately stated that the people would vote for the electors. The actual constitutional provision states that the state legislatures would decide how to choose the electors, and many state legislatures themselves appointed their electors during the ensuing years and decades.

Fourth, in response to the Antifederalist argument that the proposed Constitution would destroy the states, James Wilson and James Madison observed that the very structure of the Constitution would necessitate state governments. Among other things, the state legislatures are responsible for determining how their respective electors would be chosen.

Fifth, the proponents of the new Constitution, especially Alexander Hamilton and John Jay, emphasized the importance of the Electoral College functioning as a body of wise and knowledgeable electors who would exercise their own independent judgment in selecting the president and vice president Such electors would invariably choose a president who possessed such qualities as knowledge, wisdom, and integrity.

CHAPTER 3: THE EARLY FRUSTRATION OF ORIGINAL INTENT AND THE ADOPTION OF THE TWELFTH AMENDMENT

THE FIRST PRESIDENTIAL ELECTION

Article VII of the Constitution provided that "[t]he Ratification of the Conventions of nine States, shall be sufficient for the Establishment of this Constitution between the States so ratifying the same." Such ratification was accomplished on June 21, 1788. After that date, the following states of the original thirteen also ratified the Constitution: Virginia (June 25, 1788), New York (July 26, 1788), North Carolina (November 21, 1789), and Rhode Island (May 29, 1790).[1]

The successful ratification of the Constitution did not, however, automatically create the new government. The Congress of the Articles of Confederation was still in operation. On September 13, 1788, that Confederation Congress recognized the ratification of the new Constitution and resolved as follows:

> That the first Wednesday in January next [January 7, 1789] be the day for appointing Electors in the several states, which before the said day shall have ratified the said constitution; that the first Wednesday in February next

[February 4, 1789] be the day for the electors to assemble in their respective states and vote for a president; and that the first Wednesday in March next [March 4, 1789] be the time and the present seat of Congress [New York City] the place for commencing proceedings under the said constitution.[2]

In accordance with Article II, Section 1, Clause 3 of the original Constitution, the presidential electoral votes were counted in the presence of both the House of Representatives and Senate on April 6, 1789. George Washington was unanimously elected president. John Adams received the next-highest number of electoral votes and was therefore elected vice president.[3] Washington took the oath of office on April 30.[4]

Although it was a foregone conclusion that Washington would be elected as the first president,[5] it is important, for the purposes of the present book, to examine the mechanics of how the first Electoral College operated. Article II, Section 1, Clause 2 of the Constitution provided (and still provides): "Each State shall appoint, **in such Manner as the Legislature thereof may direct**, a Number of Electors, equal to the whole number of Senators and Representatives to which the State may be entitled in the Congress . . . ." (Emphasis added.) Only ten states appointed presidential electors in 1789. Of the original thirteen states, North Carolina and Rhode Island had not yet ratified the Constitution. New York was deadlocked between its upper and lower houses as to how the electors should be chosen, and that state accordingly failed to appoint electors.[6]

Of the ten states that did appoint electors, the legislatures of five (Massachusetts, Pennsylvania, Delaware, Maryland, and Virginia) generally directed that the people eligible to vote in their respective states should elect the electors.[7] However, this was not as simple as it might seem on the surface. In Massachusetts, the legislature determined that the state would be divided into electoral districts along the lines of the districts for the U.S. House of Representatives. The qualified voters of each district would choose one presidential elector, and the legislature would appoint two additional electors at large (for the entire state). This corresponded to the constitutional allocation of electors to each state based on the total number of its members in the House of Representatives (elected by the people) and its two senators (elected by the state legislature). But the state legislature also determined that if no elector received a majority in a district, the legislature itself would appoint the elector from the candidates with the two greatest numbers of votes. As it happened, the electoral districts failed to produce majority votes for any one candidate, and the legislature thus had to choose the district electors from the two who had received the most votes in each district. The legislature then also selected two electors for the entire state.[8] Later, when the appointed electors met on February 4 to cast their votes, they did not deliberate in the manner contemplated in Hamilton's *Federalist* No. 68 (see Chapter 2). Instead, they immediately cast their votes for George Washington and John Adams.[9]

Virginia and Delaware also had district systems for the popular election of the presidential electors.[10]

Pennsylvania and Maryland adopted a general ticket (sometimes called a winner-take-all, unit rule, or at-large system) for popular election of the electors, whereby people would vote for a general statewide slate. Federalist and Antifederalist tickets were publicized in newspapers.[11]

In four (New Hampshire, Connecticut, South Carolina, and Georgia) of the five remaining states, the legislators themselves appointed the electors. New Hampshire initially attempted a popular election of the electors, but the results did not meet the predetermined requirements fixed by the legislature, which then proceeded to appoint the electors. In New Jersey, the legislature authorized the executive branch (governor and council) to select the electors.[12]

The state governments also made various arrangements for electing members of the House of Representatives and formulating procedures for their respective legislatures to elect each state's two senators.[13]

This first election of the president under the new Constitution exhibited the problem of "double balloting," in which each elector was constitutionally required to vote for two candidates without designating which candidate was preferred for president and which for vice president. Alexander Hamilton was concerned that Washington and John Adams would each obtain an equal number of majority votes, thus triggering the contingent election constitutional provision whereby the House of Representatives, voting by states, would choose the president. Hamilton attempted to get some electors to divert their second choice from Adams to someone else in order to avoid such an embarrassing result. Although Hamilton's action was probably not, in retrospect, necessary, it pointed to a problem that would afflict later presidential elections.[14]

THE ELECTION OF 1792

By the time of the election of 1792, there were fifteen states. The state legislatures (or other state officials authorized by the legislatures) appointed the presidential electors in nine states (Connecticut, Delaware, Georgia, New Jersey, South Carolina, New York, North Carolina, Rhode Island, and Vermont). Three states (Maryland, New Hampshire, and Pennsylvania) allowed the qualified voters among the people to elect the electors by a general statewide ticket (winner-take-all). In two other states (Virginia and Kentucky), the people voted in districts for separate electors.[15] Massachusetts had a mixed system that has been variously described by the scholars.[16]

All the electors gave one of their two votes to George Washington, who received a total of 132 votes. The contest for vice president exhibited the gradual development of national political parties. The staunch supporters of the Washington administration were becoming known as "Federalists" (not the same as the former Federalist supporters of the Constitution). The followers of Thomas Jefferson and James Madison were being called "Democratic-Republicans" or "Republicans" (not to be confused with today's Republican Party). The Federalists supported John Adams for vice president, the Republicans George Clinton. Adams received seventy-seven electoral votes, and Clinton fifty. Once again, Washington would be president and Adams vice president. But the vice-presidential struggle revealed the conflict between the Federalists, who dominated in the northeastern states, and the Republicans, popular in the southern states with significant support in Pennsylvania and New York. These parties or factions did not officially nominate anyone for president or vice president in the 1792 election. Nevertheless, one scholar has observed that "[t]he results [of the 1792 election] depended on the appointment of electors already committed to particular candidates and parties." Another analysis concluded: "In most states, the choice of electors turned into a strict party contest."[17] Accordingly, we already see in this election a significant departure from the expectations of such founders as Alexander Hamilton (*Federalist* No. 68) and John Jay (*Federalist* No. 64) that the electors would independently deliberate and freely choose the president and vice president without regard to the opinions of those who had appointed them.

THE ELECTION OF 1796

After George Washington made it known that he would not run for a third term, a Federalist congressional caucus nominated John Adams as its presidential candidate and Thomas Pinckney as its vice-presidential candidate. A Republican congressional caucus picked Thomas Jefferson for president and Aaron Burr for vice president. This was the first time that national party nominations had been made for these offices. This congressional caucus procedure continued to be the way political parties nominated presidential and vice-presidential candidates until the 1820s. It confirmed the partisan nature of the process and the fact that the electors were no longer seen as exercising independent judgment in their selection of the president and vice president.[18]

The problem of the double-balloting system, whereby each elector had to cast two votes without designating who would be president and who vice president, continued to plague this election. Although the party caucuses distinguished between presidential and vice-presidential candidates, the actual ballots did not. The 1796 election involved many complicated political maneuvers that arose out of this situation. One concern was that the presidential and vice-presidential candidates of the winning party might tie, thereby sending the election to the House of Representatives. Additionally, Alexander Hamilton and some other Federalists were worried that Jefferson, their political enemy, would win the presidency. Hamilton attempted to engineer a scenario in which Pinckney, instead of either Adams or Jefferson, would win the electoral vote while obtaining a majority of all the votes. This effort failed. Adams won a majority of the electoral votes, and his number of electoral votes exceeded the electoral votes won by the second-highest candidate, Jefferson. Thus Adams, a Federalist, would serve as president with Jefferson, a Republican, as vice president. Pinckney and Burr did not obtain either of the offices.[19]

In the 1796 election, the legislatures of seven states appointed their respective electors. The qualified voters among the populace chose their electors on a general ticket in two states (Georgia and Pennsylvania). Four states (Maryland, Virginia, Kentucky, and North Carolina) provided a popular vote for the electors on a district basis. Three more (Massachusetts, New Hampshire, and Tennessee) had a mixed system.[20]

The 1796 election showed additional movement toward party identification of the electors before they were appointed.[21] The exception proved the rule. Samuel Miles, who had won election as an elector in Massachusetts after being included on the Federalist slate, decided to act in an independent manner when it came time for him to cast his vote. He voted for Jefferson, the Republican, not Adams, the Federalist. Upon learning of this turnaround, an irate Federalist voter exclaimed: "What, do I chuse Samuel Miles to determine for me whether John Adams or Thomas Jefferson shall be President? No! I chuse him to *act*, not to *think*."[22] As one scholarly study concluded:

> The rise of the caucus system destroyed forever any lingering pretense that the presidential electors . . . would be dispassionate searchers for the men of "continental character" who were fit to be chief magistrate of the republic. The founding fathers' conception of the disinterested elector vanished quietly into history, leaving its traces only in the constitution they created. Henceforth the electors would be little more than political puppets, mere tools of the political parties that had already decided on the nominees.[23]

Such were the significant consequences of the election of 1796—the first contested presidential election under the United States Constitution.

THE ELECTION OF 1800

Late 1800 and early 1801 witnessed one of the most bizarre presidential elections in American history. The events of those months demonstrated the futility and impracticability of the double-balloting rule in the original Constitution. This breakdown led directly to the Twelfth Amendment, ratified in 1804. The Twelfth Amendment cured the problem of the double-balloting rule; it did not, however, address the historical developments that challenged the very premise of the Electoral College.

The covert but protracted conflict between Hamilton and Adams, both Federalists, continued during the years of Adams's presidency. Hamilton, surreptitiously, and his

Federalist friends, openly, clamored for war with France, which was committing depredations against American shipping in the course of its continuing war with Britain. Adams, despite occasional flashes of temper, tried to maintain peace, knowing that the United States might not fare well in a military confrontation with France. But the revolutionary government in France made peace difficult, spurning Adams's emissaries and otherwise acting in an irrational manner.[24]

Hamilton had ulterior motives for war. He wanted to lead a military effort to acquire Spanish possessions in Florida and the vast western lands then known as Louisiana. Worse, during the war hysteria of 1798, the Ultra-Federalists in Congress passed the Alien and Sedition Acts in Congress. This legislation was designed in part to discourage or suppress French immigration to the United States; French immigrants often became supporters of Jefferson's Republican Party. The Naturalization Act increased from five to fourteen years the period of residence in the United States for an alien to become a citizen. The Alien Act (which Adams never used) gave the president power to deport any alien considered dangerous. The Sedition Act took aim at Republican newspapers and politicians, criminalizing "any false, scandalous, and malicious" writing against the government, either house of Congress, or the president. As a Federalist newspaper exclaimed, "He that is not for us, is against us." President Adams signed the legislation, and his administration prosecuted and imprisoned several Republicans for allegedly violating the Sedition Act. Although Hamilton initially opposed the legislation, thinking it too extreme, he wrote privately of leading a military expedition to Virginia to quell Republican opposition to the Federalists. Jefferson and Madison, the leaders of the Republican Party, did not know of Hamilton's secret plans but nevertheless were quite aware of the suppression of liberty inherent in the Alien and Sedition Acts. Behind the scenes, they prompted the Kentucky and Virginia legislatures to pass resolutions denouncing the measures. As Hamilton's military plans became clearer, both President Adams and Jefferson began referring to Hamilton as "Napoleon"—the man on horseback who was then using his military prowess to expand the French empire with the objective of taking over the French Revolution and becoming emperor.[25]

In May 1800, the Federalist caucus in Congress nominated John Adams (Massachusetts) and Charles Cotesworth Pinckney (South Carolina) as their candidates, not indicating a preference for president. The Republican caucus nominated Thomas Jefferson (Virginia) for president and Aaron Burr (New York) for vice president. The Federalist reluctance to distinguish between the two offices was probably part of a deliberate ploy by Hamilton and the Ultra-Federalists to elect Pinckney president over Adams and Jefferson. If enough southern Republican electors were to cast their second votes for Pinckney instead of Burr, Pinckney might end up with more votes than any of the other three candidates under the double-balloting rule discussed earlier. If those votes were a majority of the electors appointed, Pinckney—not Jefferson, Burr, or Adams—would become president in 1801.[26]

But this did not exhaust the possibilities. Historian John Ferling sees Hamilton as simultaneously pursuing alternative electoral strategies. First, he attempted to engineer Adams's defeat in the Electoral College. Second, he tried to put Pinckney in a favorable position by encouraging all Federalist electors to cast their two votes for both Adams and Pinckney equally. If Pinckney then obtained some southern Republican electoral votes, he might be the presidential winner. But if Adams and Pinckney tied in electoral votes while obtaining more votes than either Jefferson or Burr, the contest would go to the House of Representatives, voting by states, which Hamilton hoped would vote for Pinckney. To further these strategies, Hamilton wrote a blistering public attack on President Adams.[27]

In ten of the sixteen states, the state legislatures themselves picked the presidential electors. In five states, the legislatures arranged a popular vote. In Kentucky, North Carolina, and Maryland, the qualified voters voted for separate electors in districts. Rhode Island and Virginia had a statewide general ticket (winner-take-all) system. Tennessee employed a mixed legislative-district election system.[28]

The electoral voting in 1800 showed remarkable party discipline. Again, Professor Ferling has remarked:

Whereas roughly 40 percent of the electors had not adhered to the decisions of the party caucuses in 1796, only one elector of 138 broke ranks in 1800. It was apparent as well that the constitutional method of choosing the president had rapidly led to the emergence of party organizations, and that **as the parties crystallized, the role that the Founders had envisioned for presidential electors ebbed into oblivion** .... Instead, by the second contested presidential election, **the members of the electoral college had become the operatives of their national party.**[29]

The result of the electoral voting was, however, unexpected. Jefferson and Burr had prevailed over Adams and Pinckney with a majority of the votes, but Jefferson and Burr were tied with each other with the same number of electoral votes. Moreover, Burr declined to defer to Jefferson. Under the Constitution, the House of Representatives, voting by states, now had to choose between Jefferson and Burr for president. And the Federalists in the House were in control of this vote. Many of them wanted to make Burr rather than Jefferson president. It took thirty-six ballots, attended by many complicated political machinations, before the House finally, on February 17, 1801, selected Jefferson as the next president of the United States.[30] He took office, fifteen days later, on March 4.[31]

THE TWELFTH AMENDMENT

The first few presidential elections under the Constitution disclosed serious flaws in the Electoral College mechanism. First, the constitutional failure to require—or even allow—designation of president and vice president on the ballots of the electors resulted in such anomalies as the tie between Jefferson and Burr in 1800, thereby requiring a contingency election in the House of Representatives. Similar, though not equally problematic, possibilities were presented in the elections of 1789, 1792, and 1796. Second, the system could result in a candidate favored by one party becoming president, while the candidate supported by another party would become vice president, as occurred in 1796. Third, a minority party could make another party's vice-presidential candidate president by having its electors cast their second votes for that candidate.[32] These, and many other political machinations, affected the first presidential elections.

But such observations regarding the operation of the original Electoral College are somewhat anachronistic or presentist. The root problem was that the framers of the Electoral College did not anticipate the rise of political parties and, at the same time, overestimated the ability or willingness of the American people to make the presidential election process free from ideological or partisan considerations. "A presidential contest organized by competing parties and designed to draw in as many voters as possible was a thing the [Founding] Fathers neither planned nor wanted."[33] In a Constitution otherwise characterized by political realism, the Electoral College was something of a utopian fantasy.

By 1800, it was clear, to any objective observer, that parties were here to stay. But many still resisted this conclusion.[34]

After the election of 1796, some Federalists, unhappy with the fact that Jefferson had been elected vice president, supported a proposed constitutional amendment whereby the offices for president and vice president would be designated in the electoral ballots. In contrast, Rhode Island opposed designation because it felt that undesignated ballots gave the small states a better opportunity to obtain one of the top electoral offices.[35]

The serious procedural complications of the 1800 election, resulting in the 1801 House contingent election, stimulated Republican calls for a constitutional amendment favoring designation. In the congressional debate, several representatives of small states objected to the proposed changes to the contingent election in the House. Proponents of the amendment wanted to reduce the number of candidates in the contingent election from five to two. Opponents argued that keeping five candidates was consistent with the original intent of permitting candidates from small states to have an opportunity for the office. The latter saw the contingent election procedure, with the top five candidates, as a concession to small states in the original Constitution. Some opponents of an amendment even opposed designation itself, arguing that the original compromise in the Constitution allowed small states much more power in choosing the president. The Federalists generally were opposed to an amendment, the Republicans in favor of it. Finally, Congress approved the text of the Twelfth Amendment in December 1804, and the amendment was ratified on June 15, 1804.[36]

Under the Twelfth Amendment, as ratified, the electors are required to designate on their ballots their respective choices for president and vice president. If no person in the electoral results for president receives a majority of the votes of the whole number of electors appointed, the House of Representatives, voting by states, chooses the president from the top three candidates. If no person in the electoral results for vice president has a majority of the votes of the appointed electors, the Senate chooses the vice president from the two candidates receiving the most electoral votes.

The final text of the Twelfth Amendment, to the extent it remains operative today, is as follows:

> **The Electors shall meet in their respective states and vote by ballot for President and Vice-President, one of whom, at least, shall not be an inhabitant of the same state with themselves; they shall name in their ballots the person voted for as President, and in distinct ballots the person voted for as Vice-President, and of the number of votes for each, which lists they shall sign and certify, and transmit sealed to the seat of the**

government of the United States, directed to the President of the Senate—The President of the Senate, shall, in the presence of the Senate and House of Representatives, open all the certificates and the votes shall then be counted;—The person having the greatest number of votes for President, shall be the President, if such number be a majority of the whole number of Electors appointed; and **if no person have such majority, then from the persons having the highest numbers not exceeding three on the list of those voted for as President, the House of Representatives shall choose immediately, by ballot, the President.** But in choosing the President, the votes shall be taken by states, the representation from each state having one vote; a quorum for this purpose shall consist of a member or members from two-thirds of the states, and a majority of all the states shall be necessary to a choice. [Language superseded by Section 3 of the Twentieth Amendment is omitted.] The person having the greatest number of votes as Vice-President, shall be the Vice-President, if such number be a majority of the whole number of Electors appointed, and if no person have a majority, then from the two highest numbers on the list, the Senate shall choose the Vice-President; a quorum for the purpose shall consist of two-thirds of the whole number of Senators, and a majority of the whole number shall be necessary to a choice. But no person constitutionally ineligible to the office of President shall be eligible to that of Vice-President of the United States.

(Emphasis added.)

CHAPTER 4: THE FAILURES OF ORIGINAL INTENT FROM THE TWELFTH AMENDMENT TO THE PRESENT

DEVELOPMENTS IN THE METHOD OF SELECTING ELECTORS

State legislatures often continued to choose presidential electors, without a popular election, in the early decades of the nineteenth century. Sometimes they changed state laws for popular election of electors so as to require legislative election when they saw that such change would benefit their preferred candidate. Gradually, however, democratic pressures caused a decline in direct legislative selection of electors. Nine states utilized this method as late as 1820, but this number had declined to two states by 1828. From 1832 to the Civil War, only South Carolina used legislative election of electors, and South Carolina finally abandoned that method after the Civil War.[1] After the Civil War, the only instances of state legislative election of electors were Florida in 1868 (in the context of the postwar reconstruction of the state) and Colorado in 1876 (which had just been admitted as a state).[2]

The district method of popular election of presidential electors was never adopted by more than six states, but it remained a fixture of presidential elections until 1836, after which it came into disuse. The general statewide ticket (winner-take-all) system of popular election supplanted it, because the dominant party in the legislature could thereby suppress any minority electoral votes. Although the general ticket continues to be the predominant form of selection of electors today, Maine (in 1969) and Nebraska (in 1992) adopted modified forms of district elections that, as of the time of this writing, remain in effect.[3]

THE ELECTION OF 1824

The congressional caucus method of nominating candidates for president broke down in the run-up to the election of 1824. The Federalist Party had declined and was no longer offering national candidates. Although the Democratic-Republican Party (which had incorporated some aspects of the former Federalist national platform) remained, it was split into factions. The party's congressional congress nominated William H. Crawford, the secretary of the treasury from Georgia. But most congressional party members boycotted the caucus, and Crawford received only sixty-four out of a potential 216 votes. The Kentucky legislature nominated Henry Clay, the speaker of the House of Representatives (from Kentucky). Several New England legislatures nominated John Quincy Adams, the current secretary of state (from Massachusetts). Finally, the lower house of the Tennessee legislature, together with some popular conventions around the country, nominated Andrew Jackson of Tennessee.[4]

Before 1824 it was essentially impossible to calculate popular vote totals for the election of presidential electors, because state legislatures were so dominant in choosing the electors. In 1824, only six state legislatures chose their electors, and popular vote totals from the other eighteen states are available, though not reflective of the entire country of twenty-four states. In this election, Jackson won a plurality of the electoral votes (as well as a plurality of popular votes from the eighteen states that had popular elections). Because he did not win a majority of the electoral votes, the matter went to the House of Representatives under the contingent election provisions of the Twelfth Amendment. The House, voting by states, selected Adams, who had received the second-highest number of electoral votes (84 to Jackson's 99) for president.[5]

The election of 1824 is sometimes thought to be an example of the breakdown of the Electoral College system. But it was no such thing. The system worked procedurally exactly as the Twelfth Amendment specified. Of course, the original idea of independent electors had long since disappeared (see Chapter 3). But having received only a plurality, not a majority, of the electoral votes, Jackson was not constitutionally entitled to be selected by the House as president. Moreover, the lack of a popular vote in six of the twenty-four states makes comparison with existing popular vote tallies meaningless.

THE ELECTION OF 1876

In 1876, all states except Colorado chose their presidential electors by way of popular election in a statewide winner-take-all general ticket system. As noted above, Colorado's state legislature chose its electors because Colorado had just been admitted as a state. In the presidential election of this year, Samuel J. Tilden, the Democratic candidate, received a majority (not just a plurality) of the popular vote (not including Colorado) over Republican Rutherford B. Hayes. But the Electoral College vote was virtually a dead heat. Moreover, Congress received conflicting sets of electoral vote returns from four states. Congress appointed a special electoral commission to adjudicate the conflicting electoral votes. After protracted proceedings, including some political compromises, the commission determined that Hayes, the Republican, won the election by one electoral vote.[6]

The apparent significance of this election, with respect to the Electoral College, is that the candidate who received a majority of the popular votes cast did not ultimately receive a majority of the electoral votes and accordingly did not become president. The exact popular vote situation is not clear, however, since there were no popular votes from Colorado.

THE ELECTION OF 1888

In this election, Democrat Grover Cleveland, the incumbent president, received a plurality of the popular votes over Republican Benjamin Harrison. Nevertheless, Harrison received a majority of the electoral votes and thereby succeeded Cleveland as president.[7]

THE TWENTIETH CENTURY

At no time during the twentieth century did a presidential candidate who received the most popular votes (whether a majority or a plurality) in an election fail to obtain an Electoral College majority. The only possible exception might be the election of 1960. As a result of the strange design of the Alabama ballot (including not identifying the presidential candidates) and associated political issues involving unpledged electors, it is virtually impossible to determine whether the Alabama popular vote favored John F. Kennedy or Richard M. Nixon. Under one scenario (the one that was finally accepted), Kennedy won the Alabama popular vote; under another, Nixon did. These issues, along with questions of election fraud in some states, make it historically impossible to ascertain with certainty who won the national popular vote. Kennedy did, of course, win a majority in the Electoral College, thereby becoming president.[8]

THE ELECTION OF 2000

In the 2000 presidential election, Democrat Al Gore received 48.38% (50,999,897) of the nationwide popular vote, and Republican George W. Bush received 47.8% (50,456,002). Notwithstanding the fact that Gore won a plurality of the popular votes (543,895 more than Bush), he received only 266 electoral votes, compared to Bush's 271.[9] Bush, the winner in the Electoral College, became president.

As a result of the peculiarities of the Electoral College system, this election became enmeshed in extreme partisan conflict over the disposition of the electoral votes of the swing state of Florida. The race was very close in Florida, and the question of who won the Florida popular vote determined the assignment of the crucially important electoral votes of Florida under the winner-take-all system that all states other than Maine and Nebraska had long since adopted. Litigation ensued, and it took a decision of the U.S. Supreme Court to stop the Florida recount and declare Bush the winner of the Florida electoral votes—and, consequently, the winner of the election.[10]

Not the least of the casualties of this bizarre electoral dispute was the integrity of the Supreme Court. The politicization of the Supreme Court, which had always attended its more controversial judicial decisions, was exacerbated by this unprecedented direct foray into the procedures of a presidential election.

After Bush assumed the presidency, he governed as though he had an absolute mandate instead of a shaky victory. Successive catastrophes occurred under his watch. First, his administration evidently ignored intelligence warnings that a terrorist group planned to fly airplanes into buildings. The events of September 11, 2001, then provided the justification for the Bush administration to transform the federal government into a massive security state; the associated hysteria over terrorism also assisted Bush's 2004 reelection campaign. Second, in 2003, the Bush administration invaded the country of Iraq, which had nothing to do with terrorism, on the false pretense that Iraq harbored nuclear weapons and other weapons of mass destruction. This led to a long war, costing the United States much blood and treasure. The defeat of Saddam Hussein's Iraq upset the balance of power between Iraq and Iran, allowing Iran to have a much more powerful presence in the Middle East than it otherwise would have had. It also caused a power vacuum within Iraq, wherein terrorist groups now flourished and involved the United States in many additional years of protracted war. Third, though Democrats share some of the blame, the Bush administration and its Republican allies in Congress did little or nothing to prevent the massive fraud and speculation that led to the 2008 stock market crash and ensuing Great Recession. Finally, the administration's inadequate response to the massive hurricane named Katrina failed to attend sufficiently to the suffering of large numbers of people in Louisiana and elsewhere.[11]

In thinking about the founders' conception of the mental characteristics of a good president (see Chapters 1 and 2), Bush initially appears to be something of a puzzle. Scores on tests that are proxies for intelligence show that Bush and John Kerry—his 2004 presidential opponent, who was widely recognized as intelligent, thoughtful, and knowledgeable—were roughly equal, notwithstanding Bush's own acknowledgments that he himself was not very analytical and decided important matters by consulting his "gut." By the accounts of his close associates and others who had extensive interaction with him, Bush was intellectually incurious, impatient, impulsive, quick to anger, glib, dogmatic, evidence-averse, and ill-informed. Cognitive psychologist Keith E. Stanovich, writing at the end of the Bush administration, provided the following explanation for this apparent paradox:

> In short, there is considerable agreement that President Bush's thinking has several problematic aspects: lack of intellectual engagement, cognitive inflexibility, need for closure, belief perseverance, confirmation bias, overconfidence, and insensitivity to inconsistency. These are all cognitive characteristics that have been studied by psychologists and that can be measured with at least some precision. However, they are all examples of thinking styles that are not tapped by IQ tests. Thus, it is not surprising that someone could suffer from many of these cognitive deficiencies and still have a moderately high IQ.[12]

It is, of course, impossible to adjudicate the counterfactual of what would have occurred under a Gore presidency. But it is fairly clear that Gore would not, for example, have made the colossal blunder of invading Iraq, with all its dreadful consequences.

THE ELECTION OF 2016

In the 2016 presidential election, Democrat Hillary Clinton received 48.18% (65,853,516) of the popular vote compared to Republican Donald J. Trump's 46.09% (62,984,825). Although Clinton won a plurality of the popular votes (2,868,691 more than Trump), Trump won the Electoral College with 304 electoral votes compared to Clinton's 227.[13] Accordingly, Trump became president.

Trump has proved to be the most bizarre president in American history. He is a classic demagogue, going back at least as far as the years of the presidency of Barack Obama when he repeatedly suggested that Obama was born in Kenya and demanded that Obama produce his birth certificate. During his 2016 campaign and the months to date of his presidency, Trump continued his pattern of demagoguery, often asserting demonstrable untruths as "alternative facts." His conscious or unconscious desire appears to be the destruction of all rational thinking and discourse, especially in the political field. His speech is sometimes downright Orwellian. He frequently makes statements that implicitly or explicitly support racism and xenophobia. He contradicts himself daily, sometimes hourly. Some other presidents have been bad; none has appeared as overtly unbalanced, except perhaps when under the influence of alcohol (which Trump eschews). He has violated every norm of standard presidential conduct since George Washington. He has a total ignorance of American history and of the principles of the U.S. Constitution and government. He has repeatedly expressed a desire to

111

weaken libel laws so that he, as president, can sue his political opponents in a manner analogous to seditious libel laws that were abandoned in this country centuries ago. He wants to lock up his political opponents, especially Hillary Clinton. If he had his way, the country would become a banana republic. He has strong authoritarian impulses. While repulsing America's traditional democratic allies, he expresses admiration for blatant dictators like Russian President Vladimir Putin and Philippine President Rodrigo Duterte. Contrary to the universal consensus of U.S. governmental intelligence agencies, Trump claimed that no evidence existed of Russian interference in the 2016 presidential election. FBI Special Counsel Robert Mueller is, at the time of this writing, investigating, among other things, whether evidence exists that Trump and/or his associates conspired with the Russian government to sway the election in Trump's favor. Trump's own son, Donald Trump Jr., has admitted meeting with Russian operatives during the campaign in order to get "dirt" on Hillary Clinton for political purposes. Mueller has already obtained indictments or plea deals with some of Trump's associates that involve connections with Russia. More developments along these lines will likely occur by the time the present book has been published.[14]

The 2016 election was unique in that it triggered many of the concerns that led the 1787 Constitutional Convention to devise the Electoral College. But the current operation of the Electoral College defeats rather than accomplishes the objectives of the framers and ratifiers of that institution.

As explained and documented at great length in the Appendix and in Chapters 1 and 2, the founders thought the institution of the Electoral College would result in the selection of presidents who possessed knowledge, wisdom, experience, ability, and integrity. They believed the Electoral College would be the best safeguard against the accession of demagogues to the presidency. Additionally, the Electoral College was designed to prevent foreign powers from gaining (in the words of Alexander Hamilton's *Federalist* No. 68) "an improper ascendant in our councils. How could they better gratify this, than by raising a creature of their own to the chief magistracy of the union?" Hamilton and other framers and ratifiers of the Electoral College thought the Electoral College would thwart the success of presidential aspirants with "[t]alents for low intrigue and the little arts of popularity . . . ." Indeed, "[t]his process of election affords a moral certainty, that the office of the president, will seldom fall to the lot of any man, who is not in an eminent degree endowed with the requisite qualifications." (*Federalist* No. 68.)

The election of 2016 proved that the most important original reasons for the Electoral College are now the very reasons it should be abolished. The founders assumed that the individual electors would be wise individuals who would exercise independent judgment to choose a president who would be worthy of the position. We have seen that this underlying premise of the Electoral College was inoperative from virtually the beginning of the republic. The last chance for the operation of this original intent was

113

when the individual electors met in their separate states on December 19, 2017,[6] to cast their votes for president and vice president. Although there were some defections, the overwhelming number of electors voted the way their individual states had voted in the popular election pursuant to statewide "winner-take-all" rules. The Electoral College faced its ultimate test, and it failed. It elected a man who is the very embodiment of the kind of candidate the founders believed the Electoral College would never allow to become president. The legitimate reasons for the Electoral College have long since disappeared into the mists of American history. It is time for an alternative.

CHAPTER 5: EVALUATIONS OF THE CURRENT ELECTORAL COLLEGE SYSTEM AND PROPOSED ALTERNATIVES OTHER THAN DIRECT POPULAR VOTE

The present chapter begins by examining and evaluating the standard defenses of today's Electoral College. It then proceeds to consider the major proposals, other than direct popular vote, that have been proposed as alternatives to the existing Electoral College. The next chapter discusses the possibility of a constitutional amendment for election of the president and vice president by direct popular vote with an instant runoff voting procedure.

THE EXISTING ELECTORAL COLLEGE

For many decades, I had thought, along with many of the U.S. founders, that the electoral college was the ultimate protection against the election of a demagogue as president. As Professor Walter Berns (1919-2015) had put it,

> the issue that ought to engage our attention is the one the Framers debated over the entire course of the Constitutional Convention, namely, **what system is more likely to produce a president with the qualities required of the person who holds this great office [the presidency]? In all the years I have been engaged with this issue,**

I have yet to encounter a critic of the electoral college who argues that a president chosen directly by the people is likely to be a *better* president.[1]

In supporting his argument, Berns quoted from the July 27, 1977 testimony of Professor Herbert Storing before the Subcommittee on the Constitution of the Senate Judiciary Committee. Storing said that

> to see the case for the present system of electing the president requires a shift in point of view from that usually taken by the critics [of the Electoral College]. They tend to view elections in terms of *input*—in terms of the right to vote, equal weight of votes, who in fact votes, and the like. The framers [of the Constitution] thought it at least as important to consider the *output* of any given electoral system. **What kind of men does it bring to office? How will it affect the working of the political system? What is its bearing on the political character of the whole country?**[2]

Neither Professor Berns nor Professor Storing lived to see the election of 2016, in which the Electoral College—as distinguished from the popular vote—elected a demagogue as president (see the final section of the preceding chapter). This election proved that, at least in the twenty-first century, "a president chosen directly by the people is likely

116

to be a *better* president" than a president chosen by the Electoral College.

The Appendix and Chapters 1 and 2 of this book established that a principal purpose of the framers and ratifiers of the Electoral College was to prevent the accession to the presidency of the kind of demagogic leader that they often saw exercising power in state governments. In furthering this objective, they assumed that the persons selected as individual electors would be wise individuals who would exercise their independent judgment in choosing the president. As Alexander Hamilton put it in *Federalist* No. 68:

> It was equally desirable, that **the immediate election should be made by men most capable of analizing [analyzing] the qualities adapted to the station**, and acting under circumstances favourable to deliberation and to a judicious combination of all the reasons and inducements, which were proper to govern their choice. **A small number of persons, selected by their fellow citizens from the general mass, will be most likely to possess the information and discernment requisite to so complicated an investigation.**[3]

Citing Hamilton's rationale in *Federalist* No. 68, a recent study concludes that "[t]he Electoral College thus became our original gatekeeper" to weed out demagogues.[4] Similarly, John Jay wrote in *Federalist* No. 64:

> As the **select assemblies for choosing the president** . . . **will, in general, be composed of the most enlightened and respectable citizens**, there is reason to presume, that their attention and their votes will be directed to **those men only who have become the most distinguished by their abilities and virtue**, and in whom the people perceive just grounds for confidence. . . . **[A]n assembly of select electors possess** . . . **the means of extensive and accurate information relative to men and characters**; so will their appointments bear . . . marks of discretion and discernment. The inference which naturally results from these considerations is this, that **the president** . . . so chosen, **will always be of the number of those who best understand our national interests, whether considered in relation to the several states or to foreign nations, who are best able to promote those interests, and whose reputation for integrity inspires and merits confidence.**[5]

As we have seen in the preceding chapters, however, the electors, far from being "the most enlightened and respectable citizens," exercising independent judgment, soon became the tools of political parties, thereby defeating the original concept of the Electoral College.[6] Yet this institution, notwithstanding its signal failure to accomplish its most important objective, continues to have its defenders.

Recognizing that the principal original purpose of the Electoral College was long ago defeated, its advocates have struggled to find an alternative ground to support it and to reinterpret history to claim this alternative ground as the chief reason for the institution's inclusion in the Constitution. The new ground is federalism (states' rights), and one of the foremost contemporary advocates of this view is Attorney Tara Ross. This is the main argument of her two adult books on the Electoral College, the latest written and published after the election of 2016.[7]

Ross, like a number of her colleagues on the right, is so committed to her version of federalism that she implicitly, if not explicitly, supports repeal of the Seventeenth Amendment, which changed the method of selecting members of the U.S. Senate from state legislatures to popular election. She claims that "[p]assage of the 17th Amendment in 1913 severely harmed the interests of the states themselves. . . . . [T]he 17th Amendment, as Senator Zell Miller noted in 2004, 'was the death of the careful balance between State and Federal Government.'" "In short," Ross concludes, "states have interests, just as individuals do."[8]

Ross apparently wishes to return to one of the versions of constitutional interpretation that was prevalent in the early years of the republic: the narrow construction

119

approach of Thomas Jefferson and his Democratic-Republican Party. She does not discuss the competing broad construction of Alexander Hamilton and the Federalist Party, later adopted and applied by U.S. Chief Justice John Marshall (who had been a member of the 1788 Virginia ratifying convention). In the famous Supreme Court case of *McCulloch v. Maryland* (1819), Marshall wrote an Opinion of the Court joined by all of the other justices. In addressing the Tenth Amendment, which is a favorite reference of Ross[9] and other states' rights advocates, Marshall stated:

> Among the enumerated powers [in the Constitution], we do not find that of establishing a bank or creating a corporation. But there is no phrase in the instrument which, like the articles of confederation, excludes incidental or implied powers; and which requires that every thing granted shall be expressly and minutely described. Even the 10th amendment, which was framed for the purpose of quieting the excessive jealousies which had been excited, omits the word "expressly," and declares only that the powers "not delegated to the United States, nor prohibited to the States, are reserved to the States or to the people;" thus leaving the question, whether the particular power which may become the subject of contest has been delegated to the one government, or prohibited to the other, to depend on a fair construction of the whole

120

instrument. The men who drew and adopted this amendment had experienced the embarrassments resulting from the insertion of this word in the articles of confederation, and probably omitted it to avoid those embarrassments. **A constitution, to contain an accurate detail of all the subdivisions of which its great powers will admit, and of all the means by which they may be carried into execution, would partake of the prolixity of a legal code, and could scarcely be embraced by the human mind. It would probably never be understood by the public. Its nature, therefore, requires, that only its great outlines should be marked, its important objects designated, and the minor ingredients which compose those objects be deduced from the nature of the objects themselves.** That this idea was entertained by the framers of the American constitution, is not only to be inferred from the nature of the instrument, but from the language. Why else were some of the limitations, found in the ninth section of the 1st article, introduced? It is also, in some degree, warranted by their having omitted to use any restrictive term which might prevent its receiving a fair and just interpretation. **In considering this question, then, we must never forget, that it is a constitution we are expounding.**[10]

Marshall's analysis is reminiscent of a memorandum written by Virginia delegate Edmund Randolph at the 1787 Constitutional Convention. Randolph, who was a member of the Committee of Detail, shared this document with the Committee at an important stage of the deliberations. Randolph's paper noted that "[i]n the draught of a fundamental constitution, two things deserve attention:" First, "[t]o insert essential principles only; lest the operations of government should be clogged by rendering those provisions permanent and unalterable, which ought to be accommodated to times and events," and, second, "[t]o use simple and precise language, and general propositions, according to the example of the (several) constitutions of the several states. (For the construction of a constitution necessarily differs from that of law.)"[11]

The members of the founding generation lived in a society that largely antedated the Industrial Revolution, which brought significant improvements in communication and transportation technologies as well as the massive transformation of much of the populace from being self-employed farmers or entrepreneurs to the status of industrial wage earners. These and later technological and economic changes have rendered the present complex American society something totally beyond the imaginations of the founders. (See the epigraph at the beginning of this book.) As constitutional scholar R. Kent Newmyer has observed, "Local culture remained dominant throughout [John] Marshall's life and for much of the nineteenth century and early twentieth century as well."[12]

Moreover, slavery still existed when Marshall wrote *McCulloch v. Maryland,* and that institution was not legally abolished until after a bloody Civil War and the ratification of the Thirteenth Amendment in December of 1865. Ross does not condemn the Thirteenth Amendment. But she is remarkably ambiguous about her commitment to several other very significant constitutional amendments in her critique of the alleged devolution of the American people and society from the supposed pristine vision of the eighteenth century to a "populist mentality." She writes:

> The constitutional amendments after 1824 mirrored the increasingly populist mentality in America. The Civil War resulted in passage of the 15th Amendment [ratified 1870], which prevents states from denying minorities the right to vote "on account of race, color, or previous condition of servitude." The 17th Amendment [ratified 1913] soon followed, removing the election of Senators from the state legislatures and placing that responsibility in the hands of the people. In 1920, the 19th Amendment was ratified, ensuring that women could not be denied the right to vote based on their gender. Other changes to government were less formal, but reflected the growing populist forces nonetheless. For instance, although many state legislatures initially selected electors on behalf of their citizens, today all states hold a direct popular election for the state's electoral votes.[13]

Ross clearly expresses her opinion that the Seventeenth Amendment (popular election of U.S. senators) was a terrible idea.[14] Does she also think that the prohibition of racial and related discrimination in the right to vote (Fifteenth Amendment), women's suffrage (Nineteenth Amendment), and the popular election of the members of the Electoral College were bad ideas? From the context of her remarks, that might seem to be her position, but she refrains from explicit affirmation or denial.

And consider Section 1 of the Fourteenth Amendment (ratified 1868), which contained, for the first time, a national definition of citizenship and a general federal constitutional guarantee of individual rights against state governmental power:

> All persons born or naturalized in the United States and subject to the jurisdiction thereof, are citizens of the United States and of the state wherein they reside. No State shall make or enforce any law which shall abridge the privileges or immunities of citizens of the United States; nor shall any State deprive any person of life, liberty, or property, without due process of law; nor deny to any person within its jurisdiction the equal protection of the laws.

These two sentences fundamentally transformed U.S. constitutional law as well as the concept of federalism. Along with the Thirteenth and Fifteenth Amendments, the Fourteenth Amendment made the national government the guarantor of individual rights against **state** governmental encroachment. These amendments, passed in the wake of the Civil War and more fully implemented by the twentieth-century Supreme Court and congressional legislation, meant that the United States would never again have a hands-off policy with regard to state governmental violations of individual rights. As an eminent constitutional law scholar wrote more than eighty years ago, "[t]he most significant and conclusive constitutional decision was not rendered by a court of law but delivered at the famous meeting of General Grant and General Lee at Appomattox."[15] The Civil War and the resulting Thirteenth, Fourteenth, and Fifteenth Amendments changed everything.[16] Law professor and historian Gerald N. Magliocca has observed that "the Confederacy's defeat led to constitutional changes that were as profound as the ones launched in Philadelphia [in the 1787 Constitutional Convention]."[17]

The commitment of Ross and her colleagues to eighteenth-century federalism is, accordingly, unfounded, both historically and constitutionally. But what about her specific argument that the main purpose of the Electoral College was to protect her version of eighteenth-century federalism? That, too, is not supported by the historical evidence.

Review of the Appendix and Chapters 1 and 2 of the present book shows that although federalism was one of the founders' general considerations, it was by no means their predominant concern. In fact, as historian Gordon S.

Wood, has observed, "Many of the delegates to the Philadelphia Convention were eager to weaken if not destroy the states and the democratic excesses they had brought forth."[18] With regard to the Electoral College's framework, federalism was almost an afterthought, except for the House contingent election procedure—which has been used only in the elections of 1800 (before the Twelfth Amendment) and 1824 (after the Twelfth Amendment). The small states at the Convention realized that they would always be outvoted by the large states in the Electoral College, notwithstanding a concession in the procedure whereby each state would be allocated a number of electors equal to the total number of its senators (two) and members of the House of Representatives (variable, depending on population).[19] They believed that the Electoral College would be merely a **nominating** body, because they thought it would be difficult for one person to obtain a majority of the votes of the electors appointed. Thus, they placed their big hope on the expectation that many—if not most—presidential elections would result in House contingent elections. Since each state has only one vote in the House contingent election procedure, it would be here that the small states would seem to have a real chance of advancing one of their own candidates.[20] But it has never happened that way. Among other things, the changes wrought by the Twelfth Amendment (see Chapter 3) limited the House's consideration to the three presidential candidates receiving the largest numbers of electoral votes, whereas the original constitutional provision (which had been perceived to benefit the small states[21]) permitted the House to choose among the top five candidates without a ballot designation between president and vice president. Several small-state representatives bitterly opposed the changes made by Twelfth Amendment, but they lost. The amendment was ratified in 1804.[22]

Accordingly, Ross's history is anachronistic. She and her political allies are absolutely committed to their states' rights ideology, and they and their polemical forebears in earlier generations have long engaged in tireless attempts to impose their presentist views on the founders. One is reminded of the states' rights arguments advocated, respectively, by the Antifederalists, the antebellum defenders of slavery, and the twentieth century segregationists—all of whom lost their battles, whether literal or figurative. No one is suggesting that state governments should be abolished. As James Wilson observed on June 19, 1787, in the Constitutional Convention, "All large Governments must be subdivided into lesser jurisdictions."[23] It would be impossible—as well as undesirable—for matters of state and local government to be run from the central government. Moreover, states are protected as states in the constitutional framework for the Senate. Article V of the Constitution contains the following exception to constitutional amendments: "provided . . . that no State, without its Consent, shall be deprived of its equal Suffrage in the Senate." This is the one bedrock protection for states as states in the Constitution.

States' rights issues were quite controversial at the Constitutional Convention. Madison, James Wilson, Gouverneur Morris, and other framers fought against equal state suffrage in the Senate for months, advocating instead that both houses of Congress be based on population. But they eventually had to compromise with the small states on that issue, and we are stuck with this compromise for eternity. It is the only extant provision in the Constitution that, by its own terms, is not subject to amendment absent consent of the states. Madison considered this and related concessions to state governments to be a major defeat for his constitutional principles, but, after some private rumination, decided to soldier on, defending the Constitution that emerged from the Convention during the ratification debates and beyond.[24]

No careful reader of the Constitutional Convention debates can conclude that Madison was a defender of states' rights at this time. Indeed, he saw the state governments as the greatest threat to good government as well as individual liberty, and he accordingly wanted Congress to have constitutional power "to negative [veto] all [state] laws which to them shall appear improper."[25] In arguing for such national legislative veto power over all state laws, Madison remarked: "In a word, to recur to the illustrations borrowed from the planetary System, This prerogative of the General Govt. is the great pervading principle that must controul the centrifugal tendency of the States; which, without it, will continually fly out of their proper orbits and destroy the order & harmony of the political system."[26]

128

Needless to say, Madison's arguments for a congressional veto over state legislation did not prevail. But this was the position of the person who has been called, for centuries, "the father of the Constitution."[27]

Tara Ross concludes her 2017 book on the Electoral College with the assertion that "[h]istory has vindicated Alexander Hamilton's assessment" that "the Founders' Electoral College has proven itself 'at least excellent.'"[28] This three-word Hamilton quotation is, of course, from his *Federalist* No. 68. In context, however, Hamilton was referring not to the historical Electoral College system as we have known it but rather to his projected vision of an Electoral College wherein the electors were assumed to be individually wise and would exercise independent judgment in electing the president. (See the beginning of this section and the discussion of *Federalist* No. 68 in Chapter 2.) As demonstrated in Chapters 3 and 4 of the present book, Hamilton's concept of the virtues of the Electoral College was far removed from the actual operation of the Electoral College in the history of U.S. presidential elections.[29]

The election of 2016 has caused Ross to reflect further on her Electoral College theory. Her favorite theme is that the Electoral College losers failed to build a coalition of states in their presidential campaigns (a notion, of course, that was totally foreign to the original concept of the Electoral College[30]). Rightly or wrongly, she claims that the elections of 1888 and 2000 are examples of such failures. One could certainly argue with this premise, but the important fact for present purposes is that Ross realizes that her coalition-building hypothesis does not clearly apply to the 2016 election, in which the Electoral College winner, Donald J. Trump, "seemed pretty unconcerned about unity and coalition building. If anything, he seemed intent on the opposite."[31] In fact, Trump has governed the way that he campaigned: by appealing first and foremost to his base, with little offered to people outside his base other than vague and contradictory promises.

Ross employs right-wing media propaganda in excoriating Hillary Clinton.[32] But it is not my purpose to relitigate here the furious contest that occurred during and after the election. What is important for the purpose of the present discussion is that Ross has some sympathy for the view that Trump was unfit for office, though she has absolutely no time for the argument that Clinton "deserved the victory simply because she'd won the national popular vote."[33] As for Trump's unfitness for office, see the final section of the preceding chapter, which discusses that topic at some length. It is on this issue that Ross suggests, ever so carefully and guardedly, that the solution to this kind of scenario might be to go back to the original concept of the Electoral College in which the electors have independent judgment:

> Americans value their ability to vote and would certainly lose faith in the process if electors began to cast independent votes on any kind of consistent basis. On the other hand, many

130

> Founders considered electors to be one final
> safeguard in America's system of checks and
> balances. Perhaps modern Americans should not
> always be so quick to dismiss the possibility
> entirely.[34]

The main problem with this view, as discussed in Chapters 3 and 4 of this book, is that most Americans have never accepted the idea, expressed in Hamilton's *Federalist* No. 68 and other publications of that era, that electors should exercise independent judgment in choosing a president. It is quite unlikely that people can now be persuaded to allow such a procedure. Just imagine if a sufficient number of Republican electors had voted against Trump and caused either an outright victory for Clinton in the Electoral College or, alternatively, deprived Trump of an Electoral College majority, resulting in a transfer of the matter to a House contingent election. The Trump voters would have risen up in a fury that would have far exceeded that of Andrew Jackson's supporters after the election of 1824. It could have even led to an armed insurrection, for which the more zealous gun-rights advocates on the right have been long preparing.

Another problem with this scenario is that, once successful, it would be difficult, if not impossible, to confine it to the extreme situation of a blatantly unfit presidential candidate. Professor Robert M. Alexander, a political scientist, has authored a study demonstrating that presidential electors have been subjected to massive formal and informal campaigns—undertaken by both political parties—to persuade them to change their candidate allegiances before Electoral College votes. His book on this subject discusses statistical studies of this phenomenon in the elections of 2000, 2004, and 2008.[35] Allowing independent electors to change the result of an election could well open the Pandora's box that Professor Alexander has detected just beneath the surface of American presidential politics.

It is impossible, as well as undesirable, to return to the noble but impractical ideal of the independent elector. Today's Electoral College is clearly defective.[36] But what should replace it, and would the cure be worse than the disease? Such are the questions addressed in the remainder of this book.

DISTRICT PLAN

Several alternatives to the winner-take-all Electoral College system have been proposed over the centuries. One suggestion is that states be divided into electoral districts, with the voters in each district choosing one elector in a popular vote. In the most common version of this plan (and one that some states adopted in the early years of the republic), presidential elector districts follow the district lines for the House of Representatives in the state. One elector is elected for each district, and the two remaining electors (corresponding to that state's number of senators) are elected in a statewide vote (or directly by the state legislature). As of this writing, only Maine and Nebraska have this plan. Although states can voluntarily adopt the district system, it would take a constitutional amendment to require it in all states. Most states never adopted or, long ago, abandoned the district plan, because they found that the statewide winner-take-all procedure gave them more electoral power vis-à-vis other states.[37]

The district plan has been criticized from both the left and the right. Evidence indicates that it advantages conservative, rural voters (correspondingly disadvantaging poor and minority voters in urban areas), and this is apparently why many conservative politicians of both parties have long supported this alternative.[38] It could discourage turnout in districts that heavily favor one party or another.[39] Conservative Tara Ross points out the likely localization of issues: "Attention would be further diverted from statewide and national issues and the federal government could become even more entangled in matters that should have remained purely local."[40] Moreover, as a result of several complicated factors, the district system would not reflect the national popular vote.[41] Additionally, although the Supreme Court may decide in 2018 (after the publication of the present book) whether partisan gerrymandering is constitutional, it is possible that the Court may hold that it is not unconstitutional or that the issue is beyond the reach of the federal courts. In such case, the district plan would exacerbate the already unacceptable partisan gerrymandering of congressional districts.[42]

Individual states are free to adopt a district system, but it is not to their advantage to do so as long as most states have a winner-take-all electoral regime.[43] Accordingly, the district plan would not work on a nationwide basis without a constitutional amendment requiring it. But such a constitutional amendment has little prospect of being adopted. Absent a national convention, a constitutional amendment requires approval by two-thirds of each house of Congress plus ratification by three-fourths of the states. The larger, more urban states would have no incentive to replace the current winner-take-all electoral system with a procedure that disadvantages their voters. The last major effort in Congress for a district plan failed, during the 1950s, as a result of opposition from such large-state senators as Paul H. Douglas of Illinois and John F. Kennedy of Massachusetts.[44] The result would not be different in the twenty-first century.

PROPORTIONAL PLAN

Two basic kinds of proportional systems have been proposed. Both would abolish the state winner-take-all feature so prevalent today in presidential elections. The first proportional plan would allocate each state's popular vote for president among the whole number of electors apportioned to that state. If, for example, a state had a total of ten electors (corresponding to its two senators plus eight members in the House of Representatives) and the presidential popular vote in that state in a given election split 60.2% for Candidate A to 39.8% for Candidate B (disregarding, in this example, third-party candidates), six electors would be assigned to Candidate A and four electors would be assigned to Candidate B. In contrast, under today's winner-take-all system all ten electors would be assigned to Candidate A. The second type of proportional plan would abolish the office of elector and distribute electoral votes fractionally, depending on the popular vote in the state. For example, if a state had fifty electoral votes, it would be possible, depending on the popular vote totals, for the winning candidate to receive 38.793 electoral votes and the remaining candidate(s) to receive lower fractional numbers (the situation could be complicated by third-party candidates). This outcome contrasts with the current winner-take-all system in which the popular vote winner in that state would be assigned all fifty electoral votes.[45]

Although the first plan could be executed state by state without a constitutional amendment (as Colorado unsuccessfully attempted in 2004), such voluntary adoption is unlikely because it would reduce the electoral power of the adopting state(s) vis-à-vis the nonadopting states. Mandatory nationwide implementation of either plan would require a constitutional amendment. Proportional representation has been criticized on several grounds. It would leave intact the extra two electoral votes (corresponding to the number of each state's senators) per state while eliminating the winner-take-all system. Such a system would accordingly advantage the smaller states to the disadvantage of the larger states. For this and other reasons, proportional representation would not adequately reflect the national popular vote. It would not cure the problem of the national popular vote winner failing to become the Electoral College winner. These and other defects are elaborated in both liberal and conservative critiques of proportionality proposals. Accordingly, no constitutional amendment mandating proportionality is likely to survive congressional scrutiny (two-thirds of each house), let alone achieve the necessary ratification of three-fourths of the states.[46]

NATIONAL POPULAR VOTE INTERSTATE COMPACT

In 2001, Robert W. Bennett, a law professor at Northwestern University Law School, proposed an alternative to a constitutional amendment for a national popular vote: "State legislatures have 'plenary' power in establishing the manner of appointment of electors. There would seem to be no obstacle to a state legislature's providing beforehand that its electoral college delegation would be that pledged to the winner of the nationwide popular vote. If states with just 270 electoral votes adopted such an approach, the popular vote winner would perforce win the presidency."[47] Bennett had initially offered this proposal in January of 2001 at an academic conference on the 2000 presidential election. He later developed his ideas into a book, *Taming the Electoral College*, published in 2006. That book proposed, among other things, an interstate compact among states that would require each signing state to have its electors vote for the national popular vote winner once states having a majority of electoral votes had agreed to the compact.[48]

That same year, an entity called National Popular Vote, Inc. launched a movement with similar ideas. Its website, called National Popular Vote, is at http://www.nationalpopularvote.com. This organization has published an intensive analysis of the interstate compact concept and its alternatives in a volume of more than one thousand pages.[49] It has promulgated a text of a National Popular Vote Compact, which at the time of this writing (February 2018) has been agreed to by eleven states (including the District of Columbia, which appoints electors as if it were a state pursuant to the Twenty-Third Amendment to the Constitution) with a total of 165 electoral votes: California, District of Columbia, Hawaii, Illinois, Massachusetts, Maryland, New Jersey, New York, Rhode Island, Vermont, and Washington.[50]

Many proponents of the interstate compact plan would support abolishing the Electoral College and replacing it with direct popular vote. But they acknowledge the practical difficulties of obtaining a constitutional amendment to accomplish such a change. Instead, they have decided to work within the existing constitutional framework to achieve their objectives without an amendment. Professor Bennett has, however, observed: "As a permanent means to a popularly elected president, [the interstate compact approach] leaves much to be desired, because it skirts as many problems as it confronts. But it may have a great deal to recommend it as an interim step that would give the constitutional amendment possibility more visibility and impetus on the nation's agenda."[51]

This interstate compact proposal has generated strong opposition, especially from conservatives. In 2011, the Republican National Committee adopted a resolution opposing it.[52] Tara Ross and other conservatives have written severe critiques of the proposal, including arguments that it violates the Compact Clause of the U.S. Constitution.[53] In view of such opposition it is not clear at this time whether a sufficient number of states with the requisite number of electoral votes will ever agree to the Compact and thereby make it effective.

The National Popular Vote Compact is an exceedingly complicated mechanism that may or may not be upheld by the courts and may or may not be unwieldy in practice. If, however, it becomes effective, it may, as Professor Bennett indicated, be a way station on the way to a clearer and simpler constitutional amendment. The next and final chapter addresses this ultimate solution to the centuries-long problem of the Electoral College.

CHAPTER 6: A PROPOSED CONSTITUTIONAL AMENDMENT FOR ELECTION OF THE PRESIDENT AND VICE PRESIDENT BY DIRECT POPULAR VOTE

It may be proper to remark, that the organization of the General Government for the United States [in the Constitutional Convention], was, in all its parts, very difficult. There was a peculiar difficulty in that of the Executive. Every thing incident to it, must have participated of that difficulty. That mode [of presidential selection] which was judged most expedient was adopted, till experience should point out one more eligible.

—James Madison, June 29, 1788.[1]

In this speech in the Virginia ratifying convention, Madison was responding to James Monroe's criticism of the proposed Electoral College as making the president dependent on the state governments instead of "the people of America."[2] Madison indicated that experience might point out a "more eligible" mode of presidential selection, which, he implied, could be the subject of a later constitutional amendment. Madison certainly did not think of the Electoral College mechanism as sacrosanct. As we have seen, he had actually expressed support in the

Constitutional Convention for a system of direct popular vote.

This chapter begins with the text and an explanation of a proposed constitutional amendment for election of the president and vice president by direct popular vote. Thereafter, both advantages and anticipated objections are addressed. These discussions contain specific references to the provisions of the proposed amendment, thereby avoiding needless abstractions.

TEXT OF PROPOSED CONSTITUTIONAL AMENDMENT

The following proposed amendment for direct popular vote of the president and vice president of the United States is based on a partial amalgamation of some previously proposed amendments in Congress,[3] as modified by the present author's own conceptions. The provisions regarding instant runoff voting are based, in part, on http://instantrunoff.com/instant-runoff-home/the-basics/ (accessed February 8, 2018).

Article __

Section 1. The people of the several States and the district constituting the seat of government of the United States shall elect the President and Vice President.

Section 2. The voters for President and Vice President in each State shall have the qualifications requisite for electors of the most numerous branch of the state legislature, except that the legislature of any State may prescribe less restrictive residence qualifications and Congress may by law establish uniform residence qualifications. Congress may establish qualifications for voters in the district constituting the seat of government of the United States.

Section 3. Each voter shall cast a single vote for one slate of two persons who shall have consented to the joining of their names as candidates for, respectively, the offices of President and Vice President. No persons shall consent to their name being joined with that of more than one other person. The ballots for President and Vice President shall identify by name and party affiliation, if any, each candidate for President and Vice President on each slate. In accordance with the principles of instant runoff or ranked choice voting, each voter may rank each slate in order of preference, and the ballots and ballot technology shall be designed to permit and register such ranking. Write-in votes may be recorded in accordance with the foregoing principles.

Section 4. The slate of candidates for President and Vice President having the greatest number of votes shall be elected President and Vice

President, if such number be a majority of the whole number of votes cast. If, however, after the first round of counting, no slate has received a majority of the votes cast, the slate with the fewest votes shall be eliminated, and ballots counting for the eliminated slate shall be added to the totals of the slate ranked second on each such ballot. If no slate receives a majority of the votes cast in such second round of balloting, the process shall be repeated until one slate of candidates has a majority of the votes cast. The candidates on the slate obtaining a majority of the votes cast shall be elected President and Vice President, respectively.

Section 5. Congress shall determine the final dates for elections of the President and Vice President, which dates shall be uniform throughout the United States. Congress may also establish uniform dates for early voting and the times on each voting day in which the polls must be open. Congress shall prescribe by law the times, places, and manner in which the results of such elections shall be ascertained and declared. Subject to this Constitution, including but not limited to the provisions in this article, the times, places, and manner of holding such elections, entitlement to inclusion on the ballot, and the criteria and procedures for any state recounts shall be prescribed by law in each State; but

Congress may by law make or alter such regulations. Congress may by law provide for national recounts, if any, and for the remote possibility of a popular vote tie. Congress may by law provide technical and financial assistance to state and local governments in order to improve the security and availability of ballots and ballot technology, and Congress may by law establish uniform national standards to promote such security and availability.

Section 6. If, at the time fixed for declaring the results of such elections, the presidential candidate who would have been entitled to election as President shall have died or have withdrawn, the vice-presidential candidate entitled to election as Vice President shall be declared elected President. Congress may by law provide for the inability of such presidential candidate at such time, and Congress may by law provide for the death, inability, or withdrawal of both such candidates at such time.

Section 7. Congress may by law provide for the case of the death, inability, or withdrawal of any candidate for president or vice president before a president and vice president have been elected.

Section 8. Congress shall have power to enforce this article by appropriate legislation.

> **Section 9.** This article shall take effect one year after the twenty-first day of January following ratification.

Some details of this text might, of course, be modified during a congressional debate over a constitutional amendment, but the main principles should be retained.

EXPLANATION OF THE PROPOSED AMENDMENT

Section 1 of the proposed amendment states that "[t]he people of the several States and the district constituting the seat of government of the United States shall elect the President and Vice President." This language is taken from previously proposed amendments for direct popular vote, including one that passed the House of Representatives by a vote of 338 to 70 (82.8%) in 1969 (later successfully filibustered in the Senate).[4] It implicitly abolishes the Electoral College mechanism and substitutes the nationwide popular election of the president and vice president. Explicit repeal of the Electoral College is not necessary, as the amendments to the Constitution have proceeded by implicit rather than explicit appeal. The notable exception is the Twenty-First Amendment, which explicitly repealed the Eighteenth Amendment mandating prohibition.

Why does the text of Section 1 refer to the "people of the several States" instead of the "people of the United States"? The answer is that such United States territories as Puerto Rico are not currently assigned electors to the

Electoral College even though their people are United States citizens. One might consider that constitutional principle unjust, but allowing United States citizens resident in United States territories who are not citizens of a state or the District of Columbia to vote for president and vice president would likely expose the proposed amendment to insuperable opposition in Congress as well as in the state ratification process. If, however, Congress deems it appropriate to include citizens of territories as qualified voters for the presidency and vice presidency, it could revise this and the following section accordingly.

The text also refers to the "people of the district constituting the seat of government of the United States." As a result of the Twenty-Third Amendment, ratified in 1961, the District of Columbia "shall appoint in such manner as Congress may direct: A number of electors of president and Vice President equal to the whole number of Senators and Representatives in Congress to which the District would be entitled if it were a State, but in no event more than the least populous State . . . ." To include the people of the District of Columbia as voters for president and vice president in the proposed amendment, it is, accordingly, necessary to identify them specifically in Section 1. It should additionally be noted that the District of Columbia has no voting representatives in the Senate and the House of Representatives. A constitutional amendment would be required for authorization of the District of Columbia to have voting representatives in Congress. Although this issue is technically outside the scope of the present proposed amendment, Congress could so revise it or submit a separate proposed amendment.

Section 2 states that the voters for president and vice president in each state shall have the qualifications requisite for electors of (voters for) the most numerous branch of the state legislature. This tracks the language in Article I, Section 2, Clause 3 of the present Constitution: "the Electors [of the U.S. House of Representatives] in each State shall have the Qualifications requisite for Electors of the most numerous Branch of the State Legislature." It might be desirable to change the Constitution so as to have a nationally uniform rule regarding voter qualifications, but this is a desideratum that would likely meet with substantial opposition in Congress and in the state ratification process. Again, Congress could, if it deemed appropriate, modify this proposed amendment in such manner.

Note that the voting qualifications in Section 2 modify the word "people" in Section 1. For example, those under the age of eighteen are "people" but they generally do not have the right to vote in state and federal elections.[5]

Sections 3 and 4 contain the heart of the proposed amendment. The voter is presented with a ballot in which slates consisting of pairs of presidential and vice presidential candidates are listed. These slates are identified by political party, when applicable. The voter casts one vote for one of these slates. In accordance with the principles of instant runoff voting or ranked choice voting, the voter may also rank each slate in order of

146

preference. When the votes are counted, the initial choice of each voter is processed first. If that count shows that a majority of votes were cast for one slate, that slate is the winner, and the candidates on that slate become the next president and vice president, respectively. If, however, no slate receives a majority of votes cast on this first round, the slate with the fewest votes is eliminated, and the votes of those who voted for the eliminated slate are recast with their second choice (instead of their eliminated choice) being counted. If this second round of counting still does not result in a majority slate, the process is repeated until one slate has a majority of the votes cast. The candidates on that slate are then duly elected as president and vice president.

Section 5 allocates responsibility between the federal and state governments for election procedures and technology. Congress is required to establish uniform final days for presidential and vice presidential elections. This amendment also allows for the possibility of congressional determination of dates for early voting. To the extent not preempted by the Constitution or congressional legislation, states shall by law determine the times, places, and manner of holding such elections, entitlement to inclusion on the ballot, and the criteria and procedures for any state recounts. Congress may by law provide for national recounts, if any, and for the very remote possibility of a tie in the national popular vote. Recounts are discussed in greater depth later in the present chapter.

147

This section also requires Congress to establish procedures for ascertaining and declaring the vote. The current system could be employed, with some modifications, for such matters. Federal law might require each state to submit a certificate of ascertainment of the popular vote in its state. This information is already contained on the certificates of ascertainment submitted by the states to the federal government.[6]

Section 5 authorizes Congress to provide technical and financial assistance to state and local governments to improve the security and availability of ballots and ballot technology. This provision would authorize, among other things, federal financial assistance to states for any early voting mandated by Congress. Congress may also establish uniform national standards for ballot security and availability. As this book is being written, all of the intelligence agencies of the federal government have determined that the Russian government has interfered and attempted to interfere with the 2016 presidential election in the United States as well as elections in several other countries. Cybersecurity is one of the most important considerations in modern-day national elections, and state and local government should welcome the financial and technical assistance of the federal government for national elections.

Section 6 governs some succession scenarios not earlier addressed by the Constitution and its amendments. If, at the time the election results are declared, the presidential candidate entitled to election has died or withdrawn, the vice presidential candidate on the winning slate shall be declared president. This section also authorizes Congress to provide for the "inability" of such presidential candidate at such time and the death, inability, or withdrawal of both the presidential and vice presidential candidates at that time. The concept of inability is specifically drawn from the Twenty-Fifth Amendment. Since, however, the procedures set forth in that amendment are not applicable to a person not yet in office as president, the difficult matter of ascertaining inability is left to congressional legislation. The situation in which a president elect has died or otherwise failed to qualify is governed by Section 3 of the Twentieth Amendment. The present section does not provide for the situation in which the successful vice presidential candidate alone cannot assume office as a result of death or withdrawal. Section 2 of the Twenty-Fifth Amendment provides that "[w]henever there is a vacancy in the office of the Vice President, the President shall nominate a Vice President who shall take office upon confirmation by a majority vote of both Houses of Congress." It is contemplated that this procedure would be invoked after the president assumes office in the event the successful vice presidential candidate has died or withdrawn before the beginning of the term.

Section 7 provides that Congress may provide for the death, inability, or withdrawal of any candidate for president or vice president before a president and vice president have been elected. This function is currently fulfilled by the national political party organizations,[7] and there may be no need to change that procedure. Accordingly, Congress's authority to legislate regarding this scenario is discretionary, not mandatory.

Section 8 states that "Congress shall have power to enforce this article by appropriate legislation." Such language is included in several constitutional amendments. It permits Congress to legislate where the constitutional language is silent.

Section 9, the final section of the proposed amendment, provides that the amendment "shall take effect one year after the twenty-first day of January following ratification." Since the beginning of the term for the president and vice president is currently on January 20 of every fourth year (Constitution, Article XX, Section 1), this section allows ample time for the amendment to be in effect before the major developments in any presidential campaign.

ADVANTAGES OF THE PROPOSED AMENDMENT

Under the thumb of the current Electoral College system, we often compare the popular vote total of a candidate with that candidate's electoral vote. When a candidate wins the Electoral College but loses the popular vote, we say that the candidate is a "wrong winner." Although such a statement may be a rough estimation of reality—a heuristic, if you will—it is not quite accurate. Current presidential campaigns are waged with a view to the electoral vote,

150

especially the electoral vote of important swing states in a winner-take-all system. If the Electoral College were eliminated, the presidential candidates would undoubtedly campaign differently. Accordingly, it is, strictly speaking, impossible to ascertain what the outcome of a direct popular vote would have been had there been no Electoral College.[8]

Nevertheless, as we have observed in Chapters 4 and 5, the Electoral College has signally failed to accomplish one of its most important original objectives: avoiding the election of demagogic and/or incompetent presidents. And when we look at how the system works today in practice, it is so obviously a crazy quilt mechanism that no one in their right mind would have invented it. The founders designed an Electoral College system that had little resemblance to the current winner-take-all Electoral College. They were in their right minds, we may say, but not necessarily in their most practical minds. Viewed from the distance of more than two centuries, the founders' conception of the Electoral College was both impossibly idealistic and insufficiently respectful of the individual voter. The road to hell is paved with good intentions, and we have reached that unfortunate end of the Electoral College's long journey at the present time.

The constitutional amendment proposed above combines direct popular vote with instant runoff voting (IRV). Thomas E. Mann and Norman J. Ornstein have provided

151

the following excellent summary of the IRV procedure and its advantages:

> Voters rank candidates in order of choice, allowing ballot counts of a single round of voting to perform like a series of runoff elections. Until a candidate receives a majority of votes, ballots cast for the lowest-placing candidate are redistributed according to each voter's next choice. IRV produces majority winners, eliminates the spoiler role, and reduces the "wasted vote" calculation for minor-party candidates, allowing them to participate more fully in the election process and work to build their party's support. IRV would also complement a presidential election system based on a direct national popular vote. Building more legitimate majorities in this fashion (by eliminating the Electoral College and plurality outcomes) could well extend the electoral reach of the major parties and thereby reduce their ideological polarization.[9]

Under the current winner-take-all Electoral College system, states in which one party is dominant have relatively low turnout in presidential elections because potential voters of the minority party figure their vote will not make any difference. Presidential candidates largely ignore these states and concentrate on battleground states whose electoral votes could change the outcome of the election. In the direct popular vote scenario embodied in this proposed constitutional amendment, minority party voters in such states would no longer have a disincentive to vote. Every vote would be equal, and every vote would count. Every voter in every state would have a reason to vote, and presidential candidates would no longer focus only on battleground states. The turnout rates for presidential elections would likely substantially improve.[10]

Another advantage of direct popular vote combined with instant runoff voting is that it permits third-party candidates to make their case to the American people. Although many proponents of the Electoral College cling to its presumed strengthening of the two-party system, it is an open question whether the established Republican and Democratic parties have become too dominated by big financial interests to promote the public interest or common good. In the 2016 election, Bernie Sanders, a self-acknowledged socialist, tried but failed to obtain the Democratic nomination for president with such an antiestablishment message. Donald Trump succeeded in obtaining the Republican nomination—and then the general election—with a similar message but then predictably governed as president for the benefit of exactly those financial elites that he had pretended to oppose during the campaign. There is no reason to fear third-party movements. Historically, they have fulfilled the function in America of goading the more traditional political parties toward reforms of one kind or another. Direct popular vote with an instant runoff feature would stop any fringe candidate from becoming president. It would also prevent third-party candidates from playing a "spoiler" role in presidential elections, as Jill Stein (Green Party) and Gary Johnson (Libertarian Party) arguably did in 2016.[11]

The combination of direct popular vote and an instant runoff would ensure that each elected president would have a majority of votes, and it would correspondingly eliminate the need for a delayed physical runoff election as well as a contingent election in the House of Representatives. The instant runoff system is currently being used in many localities and some states (for limited purposes) in the United States as well as in some countries abroad. Its use in U.S. presidential elections with a system of direct popular vote would have great benefits.[12]

RESPONSE TO ANTICIPATED OBJECTIONS TO THE PROPOSED AMENDMENT

Discussions of the replacement of the Electoral College by direct popular vote often dwell on matters that belong more to the dustbin of history than with the possibilities inherent in current technology. For example, the recent availability of computerized runoff voting renders moot the longtime debate over whether a presidential candidate acquiring the most popular votes should be deemed elected with a mere plurality (less than a majority) of votes or, alternatively, whether a subsequent physical runoff election should be required. A computerized instant runoff election results in a majority vote without the delay and expense of a physical runoff election. Neither a later physical runoff election nor a contingent election in the House of Representatives (or elsewhere) is necessary. Instant runoff voting also prevents third-party candidates from becoming "spoilers" in a presidential election while allowing them an initial opportunity to test their voting power against more established candidates.

One of the main arguments against direct popular vote is that it would allegedly destroy the federalist structure of the general government. We have discussed and refuted this argument in Chapter 5. The remarks of political scientist Matthew J. Streb are also on point:

> The problem with this argument is that the founders did not adopt the Electoral College because they believed it had a federal nature; they adopted it as a compromise between large and small states, slave and free states, and because neither the option of the people nor the Congress deciding the president was appealing to the majority of the delegates [see also the Appendix and Chapters 1 and 2 of the present book]. . . .
>
> Furthermore, it is unclear exactly what the presidency has to do with federalism, since it is the only truly national office that is elected; it is congressional representation that is more in line with the notion of federalism.[13]

Issues involving fraud and recounts arise in every electoral system. The winner-take-all Electoral College is especially prone to such problems, because the candidates know in advance, through polling and otherwise, which states will be the crucial battleground states. The temptation to fraud in such cases is magnified, because the stakes are high and the dispositive opportunities are identified. In contrast, a direct popular vote system diffuses the vote over the entire country. It would be much more difficult to rig the vote over fifty states plus the District of Columbia than it is currently to do so in one or more swing states.[14] A political science professor has noted that

> under direct election, fraud and accidental circumstances can only affect the relatively few votes direct involved. Direct election would create a *disincentive* for fraud, because altering an election outcome through fraud would require an organized effort of proportions never witnessed in the United States. And because no one in any state could know that his or her efforts at fraud would make a difference in the election, there would be little reason to risk trying.[15]

Moreover, the institution of instant runoff voting would make fraud all the more difficult to accomplish. "The instant runoff further complicates the successful commission of fraud because voters express multiple preferences."[16]

The bizarre Alabama results in the close election of 1960 involved the problem of the popular ballots naming electors, some of whom were unpledged, rather than presidential candidates.[17] Such a scenario could never occur under the amendment proposed in this chapter, because Section 3 thereof states that "[t]he ballots for President and Vice President shall identify by name and party affiliation, if any, each candidate for President and Vice President on each slate." Furthermore, the Electoral College would no longer exist, and people would not vote for any intermediate electors—whether or not they were linked to particular candidates.

Section 5 of the proposed amendment contemplates that, subject to the Constitution, state law would still govern "the times, places, and manner of holding [presidential and vice presidential] elections, entitlement to inclusion on the ballot, and the criteria and procedures for any state recounts . . . ." But "Congress may by law make or alter such regulations," and Congress "may provide for national recounts, if any, and for the remote possibility of a popular tie." If allegations of fraud regarding election results surfaced in a particular state, that state could investigate the alleged fraud and, if necessary, conduct a state recount, focused, if appropriate, on a locality in which fraud was alleged to occur. In the event, however, that one or more states were found to be undertaking investigations or recounts that were dominated by a predetermined partisan agenda, the federal government could step in pursuant to congressional legislation. Additionally, state involvement in "the times, places, and manner" of presidential/vice presidential elections is subject to the Constitution, including the judicial case law disapproving election procedures that violate constitutional guarantees.

Finally, opponents of direct popular vote are fond of saying it would lead to "mob rule."[18] They evidently mean masses of people marching in the streets to demand crude redistribution of wealth. Such scenarios happened in ancient times, and some of the founders, especially Madison and Hamilton, thought they perceived such phenomena in the movements for debtor relief during the Articles of Confederation period and the associated election of demagogues to state governmental offices. But the modern political situation in the United States is much more complex. As conservative Republican commentator David Frum has observed:

> In the United States as in other countries, the great threat to constitutional democracy has not been the demands for largesse by the many, but the fears for their property of the few. The most successful antidemocratic movement in American history—the reduction of voting rights after Reconstruction—was intended precisely to thwart local majorities voting themselves such benefits as schooling and paying for it by higher taxes on the rich.[19]

Moreover, the Electoral College result of the 2016 election has given the green light to mob rule and associated political demagoguery: neo-Nazis (of whom some are "good people" according to the president) marching in the streets, presidential incitement of racism and xenophobia, a presidential order for a fascist-style military parade, presidential denigration of the FBI and other institutions of government, presidential disregard of Russian interference with our elections, the expression of presidential admiration for a Russian president who has used murder and imprisonment to eliminate political rivals, presidential praise of the systematic extrajudicial murder of alleged drug dealers instigated by the authoritarian president of the Philippines, Orwellian fake news peddled by the president and his sycophants to a propaganda echo chamber that surpasses Goebbels's wildest fantasies, and so forth. The list goes on and on and will continue to go on and on throughout the term or terms of this and perhaps subsequent presidencies.

CONCLUSION

The constitutional amendment proposed in this chapter solves the longtime problem of the Electoral College. Such a constitutional amendment will not be adopted in the near future. But a series of additional presidential elections in which the popular vote winner is not the Electoral College winner may eventually result in a constitutional amendment mandating direct popular vote. As Professor Streb has noted, "American history is full of examples of reforms that at one time seemed impossible . . . ."[20]

James Madison observed at the Virginia ratifying convention that the founders' concept of an Electoral College system (which differs substantially from our present winner-take-all Electoral College system) "was judged most expedient . . . til experience should point out one more eligible."[21] Experience has spoken. It is time to try a " more eligible" arrangement—a version of the direct popular vote plan for which Madison himself as well as James Wilson, Gouverneur Morris, and other framers expressed support in the Constitutional Convention.[22]

Appendix: A Detailed Narrative of the Debates in the 1787 Constitutional Convention on the Selection of the President

This appendix presents a detailed chronological account of the Constitutional Convention debates on the method of selection of the president of the United States, including the Electoral College. In the following discussion, most of the quotations and paraphrases are from James Madison's famous notes of the proceedings; the practice of editor Max Farrand in enclosing Madison's later revisions of his notes in angle brackets (< >) is also followed here. The notes of other delegates and the Convention Journal are also occasionally cited.[1]

The Convention delegates often used the term "executive" instead of "president." The word "president" was used more frequently after the August 6 report of the Committee of Detail.

The Convention's deliberations began on May 25, 1787, and concluded on September 17, 1787. Twelve of the thirteen states had delegations attending the Convention. Rhode Island was invited, but its legislature declined to send a delegation.[2] Each of the attending states had one vote, as in the Articles of Confederation. A state's vote was determined by the greater number of the votes of its individual delegates, but sometimes a state's vote did not count due to a tie in its individual votes. Additionally, a state sometimes could not vote because it had less than a quorum of its delegation present. For example, the state of New York had three delegates: Alexander Hamilton, John Lansing, and Robert Yates. Lansing and Yates were opposed to the emerging constitutional document, and they both left the Convention, never to return, on July 10. Being often outvoted by the other New York delegates, Hamilton had already left on June 29. Although he returned on August 13, he could not vote, because a quorum from his state was not present.[3]

Some of the debates and decisions on other matters are relevant to the issue of the selection of the president, and these proceedings are also briefly summarized here.

All dates of Convention proceedings in this Appendix and in Chapter 1 are in the year 1787.

May 29, May 30, and June 1

On May 29, Virginia Governor Edmund Randolph presented what is known as the "Virginia Plan" or "Randolph resolutions" to the Constitutional Convention. This proposal had been formulated by the Virginia delegates at a time before a quorum of states had arrived for formal deliberations. The Virginia Plan was in the nature of preliminary suggestions, and individual Virginia delegates were free to depart from the scheme to the extent they thought appropriate. Among other things, the Randolph resolutions recommended a national executive, to be elected by a national legislature.[4]

Although James Madison is often considered the principal designer of the Virginia Plan, it is not clear whether he fully agreed with all of its specifics. A few weeks before the Convention, Madison sent a letter to George Washington about general principles for a new constitution. Among other things, he wrote: "A National Executive must also be provided. I have scarcely ventured as yet to form my own opinion either of the manner in which it ought to be constituted or of the authorities with which it ought to be cloathed."[5] As will be discussed below, Madison's own statements in the Constitutional Convention revealed a preference for direct popular election of the president or, alternatively, some form of electoral college.

On May 30, the Convention resolved itself into "a Committee of the whole House to consider of the state of the American union" (hereafter "Committee of the Whole").[6] This parliamentary procedure, which was frequently used in the early weeks of the Convention, enabled the delegates to discuss issues in a somewhat informal manner. It was similar to the appointment of a committee, except that the committee in question consisted of all the attending delegates. No definitive vote was taken on any matter until after the Committee of the Whole reported to the Convention itself.[7]

On June 1, the Committee of the Whole considered Resolution 7 of the Virginia Plan: "that a national Executive be <instituted, to be chosen> by the national Legislature . . . ." South Carolina delegate Charles

Pinckney said he was for a vigorous executive but had reservations about giving that official the power of war and peace. Pennsylvania delegate James Wilson moved that the executive consist of a single person. A considerable pause ensued after this motion was seconded by Charles Pinckney. As a result of the War for Independence and the events leading up to it, many Americans had a great fear of executive power, especially monarchical power. Consequently, many state constitutions since independence had instituted plural executives of one kind or another. Most states had weak executives. This attitude was reflected in the position expressed by Roger Sherman of Connecticut: "Mr. Sherman said he considered the Executive magistracy as nothing more than an institution for carrying the will of the Legislature into effect, that the person or persons ought to be appointed by and accountable to the Legislature only, which was the despositary of the supreme will of the Society."[8]

Elbridge Gerry of Massachusetts "favored the policy of annexing a Council <to the Executive> in order to give weight & inspire confidence." Governor Randolph "strenuously opposed a unity in the Executive magistracy. He regarded it as the foetus of monarchy." After further discussion, the Committee of the Whole postponed by common consent the motion for a single magistrate. However, the Committee agreed to institute a national executive."[9]

After additional discussion of executive powers, the Committee of the Whole addressed the mode of appointing and the duration of the executive.[10]

James Wilson stated that, at least in theory, he was for an election of the executive by the people. He cited the experience in New York and Massachusetts as showing that an election of the first magistrate by the people at large was both a convenient and successful mode. He said that the objects of choice in such cases must be persons whose merits are generally known.[11]

In contrast, Connecticut delegate Roger Sherman supported appointment of the executive by the national legislature and making that official absolutely dependent upon the legislature. "An independence of the Executive on [from] the supreme Legislative, was in his opinion the very essence of tyranny if there was any such thing."[12]

James Wilson **"renewed his declarations in favor of an appointment by the people. He wished to derive not only both branches of the Legislature from the people, without the intervention of the State Legislatures <but the Executive also;> in order to make them as independent as possible of each other, as well as of the States."**[13]

George Mason of Virginia said he favored the idea of popular election of the executive but thought it impracticable.[14] Delegate John Rutledge (South Carolina) suggested that the second branch of the legislature (what would become the Senate) should alone elect the executive.[15]

June 2

Charles Pinckney supported the election of the executive by the national legislature. That mode of selection would ensure that "respect will be paid to that character best qualified to fill the Executive department of Government."[16]

James Wilson moved to postpone Randolph's proposal that the executive be chosen by the national legislature in order to take up his own new resolution that the states be divided into districts and that the persons qualified to vote in each district elect members for their respective districts to be electors of the executive. Wilson argued that the election of the executive should proceed without the intervention of the states. He claimed that his suggested mode of election would produce more confidence in the first magistrate among the people than an election by the national legislature.[17]

Elbridge Gerry of Massachusetts opposed the election of the executive by the national legislature. He said this would result in a constant intrigue kept up for the appointment. The legislature and the candidates would bargain and play into one another's hands. Votes would be given by the former under promises or expectations from the latter, of recompensing them by services to members of the legislature or to their friends. Although he liked the principle of Wilson's motion, he feared that it would be opposed by partisans of the state governments as tending to supersede altogether the state authorities. He thought that people were not ready for such a step and that such proposal should be postponed until the people felt more the necessity of it. He seemed to prefer the taking the suffrages of the states instead of electors, or letting the state legislatures nominate and the electors appoint. In Madison's words, Gerry was "not clear that the people ought to act directly even in <the> choice of electors, being too little informed of personal characters in large districts, and liable to deceptions."[18]

Hugh Williamson of North Carolina stated that he could see no advantage in the introduction of electors chosen by the people, who would then stand in the same relation to them as to the state legislatures, while this expedient would be attended with great trouble and expense.[19]

At the conclusion of this debate on June 2, Wilson's electoral college scheme was defeated. The proposal for electing the executive by the national legislature for a term of seven years was approved.[20]

June 7

The Virginia Plan had proposed that the second house (Senate) of the national legislature be elected by the first (House of Representatives).[21] On June 7, the Committee of the Whole voted to replace this provision with the election of the second house by the state legislatures. It was not, however, determined whether the allocation of senators was to be based on population or on equality of states.[22]

June 8-9

On June 8, James Madison seconded a motion by Charles Pinckney that the national legislature should "have authority to negative [veto] all [state] Laws which they shd. judge to be improper." Having seen how state governments had rendered the Congress of the Articles of Confederation impotent to deal with any significant issue, Madison argued strongly that "[t]his prerogative of the General Gov[ernmen]t is the great pervading principle that must controul the centrifugal tendency of the States; which, without it, will continually fly out of their proper orbits and destroy the order & harmony of the political system." Pinckney's motion was, however, defeated by a vote of three ayes (Massachusetts, Pennsylvania, Virginia), seven noes, and one divided (Delaware).[23]

On the same date, Gerry successfully moved to reconsider the June 2 affirmative vote of the Committee of the Whole regarding the appointment of the national executive by the national legislature.[24] On June 9, he proposed that "the National Executive should be elected by the Executives of the States whose proportion of votes should be the same with that allowed to the States in the election of the Senate." (See the June 7 entry, above.) Gerry argued that appointment by the national legislature could lessen the national executive's independence and give birth to intrigue and corruption between the executive and the legislature previous to the election as well as partiality in the executive afterward to the latter's supporters in the legislature. Gerry thought, in Madison's words, that the states' executives "would be mostly likely to select the fittest men, and that it would be their interest to support the man of their own choice."[25]

Randolph opposed Gerry's motion, citing a number of reasons, and the motion was rejected.[26]

June 13

The Committee of the Whole reported its determinations regarding the Virginia Plan to the Convention. The report included a recommendation that a national executive be chosen by the national legislature for a term of seven years with an ineligibility to serve a second term.[27]

June 14

William Paterson of New Jersey requested a postponement of the Convention's consideration of the report from the Committee of the Whole to permit New Jersey and some other states to prepare a competing proposal. The Convention adjourned in order to accommodate Paterson and his associates.[28]

June 15

William Paterson presented what is known as the "New Jersey Plan." Among other things, this proposal included a provision that the federal executive be elected by the Congress. Paterson evidently meant the unicameral Confederation Congress, as he did not propose anything like the bicameral bodies that became the House of Representatives and the Senate. The Convention referred these propositions to the Committee of the Whole and also recommitted the report of the Committee of the Whole on the Virginia Plan back to the Committee.[29]

June 18

In the Committee of the Whole, New York delegate Alexander Hamilton gave an extended speech in which he outlined his own plan for the new government. He supported a strong executive. He believed the British government, including its hereditary king, was the best in the world. He recommended that the executive authority of the United States be vested in a governor to be elected to serve during good behavior. The election, he thought, should be made by electors chosen by the people in election districts.[30]

July 12

On this date, the Convention adopted the so-called Three-Fifths Compromise for representation and direct taxation, whereby each free inhabitant would be counted as one person and each slave would be counted as three-fifths of a person.[31] The Convention had not yet decided whether both houses of the national legislature would be based on population. As later incorporated into Article I, Section 2, Clause 3 of the original Constitution, the Three-Fifths Clause, which by then applied only to elections for the House of Representatives, provided that "Representatives and direct Taxes shall be apportioned among the several States ... according to their respective Numbers, which shall be determined by adding to the whole Number of free Persons, including those bound to Service for a Term of Years, and excluding Indians not taxed, three-fifths of all other Persons." This language was modified by Section 2 of the Fourteenth Amendment, ratified on July 9, 1868, which stated in pertinent part: "Representatives shall be apportioned among the several States according to their respective numbers, counting the whole number of persons in each State, excluding Indians not taxed."

July 16

On July 16, the Convention adopted what became known as the Great Compromise or Connecticut Compromise. The composition of the first branch (which became the House of Representatives) of the national legislature was to be based on population (with three-fifths of each slave being counted for purposes of apportionment). In contrast, each state would have an equal representation in the second branch (which became the Senate). The delegates from the larger states, including James Madison, bitterly opposed making the Senate based on equal state representation as distinguished from population. The vote was five states (Connecticut, New Jersey, Delaware, Maryland, and North Carolina) in favor and four states (Pennsylvania, Virginia, South Carolina, and Georgia) against this compromise plan. The delegates from Massachusetts were divided, the delegates from New York were absent, the New Hampshire delegation had not yet arrived, and Rhode Island did not attend the Convention. Notwithstanding the continuing discontent of Madison and other delegates from large states, the so-called Great Compromise was not later altered, and it became a permanent part of the Constitution.[32]   Indeed, Article V of the Constitution, governing constitutional amendments, stipulates that "no State, without its Consent, shall be deprived of its equal Suffrage in the Senate."

July 17

The Convention debated a clause of a resolution reported from the Committee of the Whole whereby the national legislature would have power "to negative all laws passed by the several States contravening, in the opinion of the national legislature, the articles of union, or any treaties subsisting under the authority of the Union."   James Madison argued strongly in favor of such a national negative on state laws as being essential to the efficacy and security of the general government.   However, the Convention rejected this proposition, with only Massachusetts, Virginia, and North Carolina voting for it.[33] Instead, the Convention unanimously agreed to a resolution by Luther Martin that later was substantially incorporated into what became the Supremacy Clause (Article VI, Section 2) of the U.S. Constitution.[34]

The Convention unanimously agreed that the national executive should consist of a single person.[35]

The Convention passed a motion that the executive should be chosen by the national legislature and rejected motions providing for the election of the executive by the citizens of the United States and by electors appointed by the state legislatures.[36] The following significant debate preceded these votes.

Gouverneur Morris (Pennsylvania) opposed the election of the national executive by the national legislature, stating that the executive would then be a mere creature of the legislature. "**He ought to be elected by the people at large,** by the freeholders of the Country. That difficulties attend this mode, he admits." But Morris argued that such difficulties had been overcome in the instances of New York and Connecticut and would similarly be overcome in the case of the popular election of an executive for the United States. "If the people should elect, they will never fail to prefer some man of distinguished character, or services; some man, if he might so speak, of continental reputation." On the contrary "[i]f the Legislature elect, it will be the work of intrigue, of cabal, and of faction ... ; real merit will rarely be the title to the appointment."[37]

Connecticut delegate Roger Sherman thought that the sense of the nation would be better expressed by the national legislature, as distinguished from the people at large. "The latter will never be sufficiently informed of characters, and besides will never give a majority of votes to any one man." He argued that the people "will generally vote for some man in their own State, and the largest State will have the best chance for the appointment."[38]

James Wilson responded in some detail to some of the particular arguments against the popular election of the executive. To him, an important objection against an absolute election of the executive by the legislature was that the executive in that case "would be too dependent to stand the mediator between the intrigues & sinister views of the Representatives and the general liberties & interests of the people."[39]

Charles Pinckney of South Carolina argued that an election of the executive by the people was "liable to the most obvious & striking objections. They will be led by a few active & designing men. The most populous States by combining in favor of the same individual will be able to carry their points." He concluded that the national legislature, "being most immediately interested in the laws made by themselves, will be most attentive to the choice of a fit man to carry them properly into execution."[40]

Gouverneur Morris disagreed. "It is said that in case of an election by the people the populous States will combine & elect whom they please. Just the reverse. The people of such States cannot combine. If their [*sic*] be any combination it must be among their representatives in the Legislature." As to the argument that the people will be led by a few designing men, "This might happen in a small district. It can never happen throughout the continent." Morris also objected to the assertion that the people would be too uninformed to make a wise selection of the executive. He responded that "they will not be uninformed of those great & illustrious characters which have merited their esteem & confidence." After reviewing historical examples of "usurpation & tyranny on the part of the

Legislature" in selecting the executive, he concluded that "[a]ppointments made by numerous bodies [i.e., legislatures] are always worse than those made by single responsible individuals, or by the people at large."[41]

George Mason of Virginia suggested that the popular election of the executive would be impracticable: "He conceived it would be as unnatural to refer the choice of a proper character for chief Magistrate to the people, as it would, to refer a trial of colours to a blind man. The extent of the Country renders it impossible that the people can have the requisite capacity to judge of the respective pretensions of the Candidates."[42]

James Wilson repeated his opposition to the legislative appointment of the executive, concluding that it was notorious that this branch of business "was most corruptly managed of any that had been committed to legislative bodies."[43]

Hugh Williamson of North Carolina argued against the popular election of the executive. "There are at present distinguished characters, who are known perhaps to almost every man. This will not always be the case. The people will be sure to vote for some man in their own State, and the largest State will be sure to succede [succeed]. This will not be Virga. however. Her slaves will have no suffrage."[44] Williamson here let the cat out of the bag. Virginia was the largest state in population, if one counted slaves, but that state did not have the greatest number of people eligible to vote. Accordingly, a system of direct popular vote would be less advantageous to Virginia than a system that somehow factored in the total population of each state regardless of the number of persons admitted to the franchise. We shall see that Madison picked up this theme a couple of days later.

The states present at the Convention then voted against election of the executive by the citizens of the United States, against election of the executive by electors chosen by the state legislatures (only Delaware and Maryland voted in favor of this motion), and for appointment of the executive by the national legislature (unanimous vote in favor). Pennsylvania was the sole state to vote in favor of election by the people.[45] Although it is unknown how the individual Pennsylvania delegates voted, it is significant that this delegation of eight individuals included Benjamin Franklin, James Wilson, and Gouverneur Morris. One scholar has observed that Pennsylvania "boasted a hefty, fast-growing population and imposed virtually no property qualifications on its voters. In any system of direct election, such a state would loom large . . . ."[46]

Luther Martin of Maryland then moved that the executive be chosen by electors appointed by the several legislatures of the individual states. This motion was rejected by eight states to two. Only Delaware and Maryland voted in favor of this mode of election.[47]

The Convention then unanimously agreed to the procedure that the national executive should be chosen by the national legislature.[48] This, of course, was not the final determination.

July 19

Gouverneur Morris restated his support for popular election of the executive. He argued that the executive should be appointed by the people because **"the Executive Magistrate should be the guardian of the people, even of the lower classes, agst. Legislative tyranny, against the Great & the wealthy who in the course of things will necessary compose—the Legislative body. Wealth tends to corrupt the mind & to nourish its love of power, and to stimulate it to oppression. History proves this to be the spirit of the opulent."** Accordingly, the executive **"ought to be so constituted as to be the great protector of the Mass of the people."** Morris "saw no alternative for making the Executive independent of the Legislature but either to give him his office for life, or make him eligible by the people."[49]

Edmund Randolph "thought an election by the [national] Legislature with an incapacity to be elected a second time would be more acceptable to the people tha[n] the plan suggested by" Gouverneur Morris. Randolph thought such ineligibility for reelection would prevent undue influence by the legislature over the executive.[50]

Massachusetts delegate Rufus King disliked any ineligibility of the executive to be elected for a second term. "He was much disposed to think that in such cases the people at large would chuse wisely. There was indeed some difficulty arising from the improbability of a general concurrence of the people in favor of one man. On the whole, he was of opinion that an appointment by electors chosen by the people for the purpose, would be liable to fewest objections."[51]

William Paterson's ideas "nearly coincided he said with those of Mr. King. He proposed that the Executive should be appointed by Electors to be chosen by the States in a ratio that would allow one elector to the smallest and three to the largest states."[52]

James Wilson observed that, in the words of Madison, "[i]t seems to be the unanimous sense that the Executive should not be appointed by the [national] Legislature, unless he be rendered in-eligible a 2d time: **he perceived with pleasure that the idea was gaining ground, of an election mediately or immediately by the people.**"[53]

At this juncture James Madison made an important speech on the question. He emphasized the importance not only of the separation but also the independence of the executive from the legislature. He disagreed with the Virginia Plan's proposal of appointment of the national executive by the national legislature. Since the Virginia Plan is thought by many scholars to have been primarily the work of Madison, this may have been a significant transformation in his thinking. If Madison changed his mind on this subject, he may have been motivated by his disenchantment with the recently adopted "Great Compromise" whereby each state would have equality of representation in the Senate. If one of two houses of the national legislature was going to be controlled by the small states, Madison may have thought some other mechanism should be found for selection of the president.[54] He might also have been influenced by the speeches of those delegates who had been pointing out the dangers of having the executive dependent on the legislature. Madison now observed:

> Certain it was that the appointment [of the executive by the national legislature] would be attended by intrigues and contentions that ought not to be unnecessarily admitted. **The people at large was in his opinion the fittest in itself. It would be as likely as any that could be devised to produce an Executive Magistrate of distinguished Character. The people generally could only know & vote for some Citizen whose merits had rendered him an object of general attention & esteem. There was one difficulty however of a serious nature attending an immediate choice by the people. The right of suffrage was much more diffusive in the Northern than the Southern States; and the latter could have no influence in the election on the score of the Negroes. The substitution of electors obviated this difficulty and seemed on the whole to be liable to the fewest objections.**[55]

Accordingly, Madison favored popular election of the executive as filtered through an electoral college; he was **not**, however, supporting selection of electors by state legislatures or state executives.[56] This is consistent with

Madison's general distrust of state governments at the time of the Convention, including his opposition to equal state representation in what became the Senate and his desire for a national veto over state legislation. Madison's expression of confidence in the people was unusual (albeit shared with a few other delegates), but his concern for protecting the political interests of the slaveholding states was widely shared by the southern delegates to the Convention. One historian has explained the southern thought process as follows:

> There was little sentiment for popular election— for all the talk of democracy, this was not a group that had a good deal of trust in the common man. . . . No one, however, opposed popular election more vehemently than the southerners. Although the southern states had obtained legislative apportionment for three-fifths of its slaves, that formula would not be applied in a popular vote for the executive. A man who owned a slave would not get 1.6 votes, nor would 60 percent of the slaves be allowed to line up at the ballot box. If election were by popular vote, presidents (except perhaps Washington, whom just about everyone assumed would hold the office initially) would most certainly come from the North until such time as the South could secure a majority of the white population.[57]

But what did Madison mean when he said that the "substitution of electors" would obviate the "difficulty" arising from the fact that the right of suffrage was "more diffusive in the Northern than in the Southern States"? We may discern Madison's thinking by considering Hugh Williamson's proposal the very next day that electors should be apportioned to each state in future elections on the basis of the allocation of representatives to such state in the first house (House of Representatives) of the legislature. In accordance with the July 12 Three-Fifths Compromise and the July 16 Great Compromise, this allocation of representatives was based on the nonslave population of the state (not including Native Americans not taxed) plus three-fifths of that state's slaves. One wonders whether Madison had already discussed this with Williamson before making the remark that the substitution of electors would obviate the difficulty accruing to the southern states in a popular vote scenario. Although Williamson's motion was not seconded and was not the subject of a vote, it became the kernel for the ultimate determination of this issue.[58]

In the meantime, however, Elbridge Gerry suggested an electoral scheme that went nowhere. On July 19, immediately after Madison's speech, Gerry stated:

> **The people are uninformed, and would be misled by a few designing men. He urged the expediency of an appointment of the Executive by Electors to be chosen by the State Executives.** The people of the States will

then choose the 1st branch [the House of Representatives]: The legislatures of the States the 2nd. branch [Senate] of the National Legislature, and the Executives of the States, the National Executive – This he thought would form a strong attachnt. in the States to the National System. The popular mode of electing the chief Magistrate would certainly be the worst of all.[59]

The Convention then voted to reconsider the method of selecting the executive. Oliver Ellsworth of Connecticut moved to strike out the appointment of the executive by the national legislature and to insert the words "to be chosen by electors appointed by the Legislatures of the States" in the following ratio: one for each state not exceeding 200,000 inhabitants, two for each above that number and not exceeding 300,000, and three for each state exceeding 300,000 inhabitants.[60] Ellsworth specifically used the word "inhabitants" rather than any term referring to those admitted to the franchise. Perhaps this was designed to appeal to the southern states, since "inhabitants" would include nonvoting slaves. But Ellsworth's proposal was not adopted. As Madison observed the next day, that formula would, in time, make all or nearly all the states equal, because there were few that would not eventually "contain the number of inhabitants entitling them to 3 Electors . . . ."[61]

Although Elbridge Gerry agreed with the procedure of using electors, he suggested a somewhat different method of allocating them among the states: Massachusetts, Pennsylvania, and Virginia would each have three electors; Connecticut, New York, New Jersey, Maryland, North Carolina, and South Carolina would each have two; and New Hampshire, Rhode Island, Delaware, and Georgia would each have one. Additionally, he repeated his desire that the electors be appointed by the state executives. Nevertheless, he preferred Ellsworth's procedure (whereby the state legislatures would choose the electors) over the alternative modes of their appointment by the national legislature or by the people.[62]

John Rutledge of South Carolina said he was opposed to any mode of election of the executive other than appointment by the national legislature, and he thought that the only way the executive could be sufficiently independent of the legislature was to be ineligible for a second term.[63] Note that appointment of the executive by the national legislature would be somewhat protective of southern interests as a result of the July 12 decision in which slaves were to be counted as three-fifths of a person for legislative apportionment and the July 16 Great Compromise in which the first branch (House of Representatives) of that legislature would be subject to the three-fifths provision because it would be based on population.

The Convention adopted Ellsworth's proposal that the executive should be appointed by electors chosen by the state legislatures. The question of the ratio whereby the electors were to be allocated among the states was postponed. The Convention voted against making the executive ineligible for reelection and also rejected a seven-year term for that office. However, it approved a six-year term for the executive.[64]

July 20

Elbridge Gerry's July 19 proposal regarding the apportionment of electors in the first election was approved. As mentioned above, Hugh Williamson moved that electors in future elections be apportioned among the states by their respective numbers of representatives in the House of Representatives, but this motion was not seconded and no vote was taken on it.[65]

July 21

It was unanimously agreed that the electors of the executive should be paid out of the national treasury for the devotion of their time to public service.[66] This provision was not, however, contained in the final version of the Constitution.

July 23

Delegates from New Hampshire arrived at the Convention for the first time and took their seats.[67] The Convention now had delegates from eleven of the thirteen states. Rhode Island never sent any delegates, and the delegates from New York had left the Convention. Although no New Jersey delegates voted on July 21 and 23, New Jersey delegates were present and voting on July 20 and 24.[68]

The Convention agreed to reconsider, the next day, the appointment of the executive by electors chosen by the state legislatures. It also agreed that "the proceedings of the Convention for the establishment of a national government, except what respects the Supreme Executive, be referred to a Committee for the purpose of reporting a Constitution conformably to the Proceedings aforesaid" and that such committee (later called the Committee of Detail) should consist of five delegates, to be selected the following day.[69]

July 24

Just when it seemed to be settled that the executive would be chosen by electors appointed by the state legislatures, the Convention reversed itself and, by a vote of seven to four (Connecticut, Pennsylvania, Maryland, and Virginia dissenting), went back to the formerly discarded idea of the executive being appointed by the national legislature. This put the Convention into turmoil, including debate over various schemes to mitigate executive-legislative intrigue. The session concluded with the appointment of delegates John Rutledge (South Carolina), Edmund Randolph (Virginia), Nathaniel Gorham (Massachusetts), Oliver Ellsworth (Connecticut), and James Wilson (Pennsylvania) to the Committee of Detail.[70]

July 25

The Convention again took up the question of the selection of the executive. Oliver Ellsworth of Connecticut moved for the following amendment to the resolution passed on July 24 that the executive be appointed by the national legislature: "except when the Magistrate last chosen shall have continued in office the whole term for which he was chosen, and be reeligible in which case the choice shall be by Electors appointed for that purpose by the several [state] legislatures." This proposed amendment was rejected by a vote of seven noes to four ayes. In the discussion leading up to this vote, however, some of the delegates made some important points.[71]

Elbridge Gerry (Massachusetts) repeated his remark that an election by the national legislature "was radically and incurably wrong," and he moved that the executive be appointed by the governors and presidents of the states, with advice of their executive councils, and, when there are no councils, by electors chosen by the state legislatures. This motion evidently lacked a second, since the Journal does not even mention it and records no vote on it.[72]

James Madison then gave a significant speech on these issues. He surveyed the possible modes of selecting the executive. He began with the resolution adopted the preceding day whereby the national legislature was to appoint the executive. Madison considered this procedure to be "liable to insuperable objections." He observed that it would generally impinge on the independence of the executive. He also had three specific objections. First, such a procedure "would agitate & divide the [national] legislature so much that the public interest would materially suffer by it." Second, "the candidate would intrigue with the Legislature, would derive his appointment from the predominant faction, and be apt to render his administration subservient to its views." Finally, **"[t]he Ministers of foreign powers would have and make use of, the opportunity to mix their intrigues & influence with the Election."** Madison argued that selection of the executive "will be an object of great moment with the great rival powers of Europe who have American possessions, to have at the head of our Governmt. a man attached to their respective politics & interests. No pains, nor perhaps expence, will be spared, to gain from the Legislature an appointmt. favorable to their wishes." He cited the examples of foreign interference in the executive elections of Germany and Poland.[73]

Madison then addressed the possibility of an appointment of the national executive by the executives or legislatures of the state governments. He noted that some of the arguments against selection of the national executive by state executives (state governors or presidents) had already been mentioned. He added that state executives "could & would be courted, and intrigued with by the Candidates, by their partizans, and by the Ministers of foreign powers." Madison was adamantly opposed to selection of the national executive by state legislatures. Implicitly referencing state developments under the Articles of Confederation, including the adoption by state legislatures of paper money, Madison argued that "[t]he Legislatures of the States had betrayed a strong propensity to a variety of pernicious measures." Still hoping for a national veto power ("negative") over state laws, Madison continued: "One object of the Natl. Legislre. was to controul this propensity. One object of the Natl. Executive, so far as it would have a negative on the [state] laws, was to controul the Natl. Legislature, so far as it might be infected with a similar propensity. Refer the appointmt of the Natl. Executive to the State Legislatures, and this controuling purpose may be defeated. The [state] legislatures can & will act with some kind of regular plan, and will promote the appointmt. of a man who will not oppose himself to a favorite object. Should a majority of the [state] Legislatures at the time of election have the same object, or different objects of the same kind, the Natl Executive, would be rendered subservient to them."[74]

Having disposed of the election of the national executive by both the national legislature and the states legislatures or executives, Madison concluded that the remaining options were an appointment by electors chosen by the people or an immediate appointment by the people. "He thought the former mode free from many of the objections which had been urged agst it, and greatly preferable to an appointment by the Natl. Legislature. As the electors would be chosen for the occasion, would meet at once, & proceed immediately to an appointment, there would be very little opportunity for cabal, or corruption." Evidently assuming that the electors would all meet in one place, Madison said "[a]s a further precaution, it might be required that they should meet at some place, distinct from the seat of Govt. and even that no person within a certain distance of the place at the time shd. be eligible." He evidently meant eligible for appointment as the national executive. He concluded, however, that this mode of election of the national executive "had been rejected so recently & by so great a majority that it probably would not be proposed anew."[75]

Madison then discussed what appeared to him to be the remaining option:

> **The remaining mode was an election by the people** or rather by the <qualified part of them>[[76]] at large. **With all its imperfections he liked this best.** He would not repeat either the general argumts. for or the objections agst this mode. He would only take notice of two difficulties which he admitted to have weight. The first arose from the disposition in the people to prefer a Citizen of their own State, and the disadvantage this wd. throw on the smaller States. Great as this objection might be he did not think it equal to such as lay agst. every other mode which had been proposed. He thought too that some expedient might be hit upon that would obviate it. The second difficulty arose from the disproportion of <qualified voters> in the N. & S. States, and the disadvantages which this mode would throw on the latter. The answer to this objection was: 1. that this disproportion would be continually decreasing under the influence of the Republican laws introduced in

189

the S. States, and the more rapid increase of their population,   2. That local considerations must give way to the general interest.   As an individual from the S. States he was willing to make the sacrifice.[77]

The disproportion of qualified voters in the northern and southern states implicitly referred to the fact that slaves were not allowed to vote in the southern states.   It is interesting that Madison assumed that this disproportion would decrease under the influence of republican laws introduced in the southern states.   We now know, of course, that the slavery regime became more, not less, entrenched in the laws of the southern states during the decades before the ratification, in late 1865, of the Thirteenth Amendment after the conclusion of the Civil War.   Madison and many others at this time also assumed that the southern white population would increase more rapidly than northern population.   That did not happen.   Madison's final comment that "local considerations must give way to the general interest" and that, as a southerner, he was "willing to make the sacrifice" may have been in the nature of a wake-up call to rouse the other southern delegates to get behind an electoral college plan.

Ellsworth concluded the discussion of his proposed amendment described at the beginning of this section with a comment that "[t]he objection drawn from the different sizes of the States, is unanswerable.   The Citizens of the largest States would invariably prefer the Candidate within the State: and the largest States wd. invariably have the man." Thereafter, Ellsworth's motion was defeated.[78]

Charles Pinckney now moved that the election of the executive by the national legislature be qualified with a proviso that no person be eligible for more than six years in any twelve years. He thought this would have all the advantages, while mitigating the inconveniences, of an absolute ban on the executive being elected for a second term.[79]

George Mason approved this idea. He observed that it had the sanction of experience in the instance of the Confederation Congress and in the practices of some states. He generally preferred the election of the national executive by the national legislature, though he admitted that "there was great danger of foreign influence, as had been suggested. This was the most serious objection with him that had been urged."[80]

Pierce Butler stated that "[t]he two great evils to be avoided are cabal at home, & influence from abroad. It will be difficult to avoid either if the Election be made by the national legislature. On the other hand, the Govt. should not be made so complex & unwieldy as to disgust the States. This would be the case, if the election shd. be referred to the people." Butler "liked best an election by Electors chosen by the Legislatures of the States. He was agst. a re-eligibility [of the executive for a second term] at all events." He also favored an equality of states (rather than electors being apportioned on the basis of population).[81]

Elbridge Gerry approved of Pinckney's motion "as lessening the evil."[82]

Pinckney's proposal involved what was called "rotation in office," a practice familiar to the delegates as a result of its use under the Articles of Confederation and in some state governments. Gouverneur Morris said that he "was agst. a rotation in every case. It formed a political School, in wch. we were always governed by the scholars [students], and not by the Masters [teachers]." He observed that "[t]he evils to be guarded agst in this case are[:] 1. the undue influence of the Legislature[,] 2. instability of Councils[,] 3. misconduct in office. To guard agst. the first, we run into the second evil.... A change of men is ever followed by a change of measures." Morris, a delegate from Pennsylvania, used that state as an example of the "vicissitudes among ourselves...." He argued further that "the Rotation in office will not prevent intrigue and dependence on the Legislature. The man in office will look forward to the period at which he will become re-eligible." During the interim years, he might become a member of the national legislature. This prospect will cause him to be careful, during his first executive term, not to oppose the expansion of legislative power, and he "will be very unwilling to take any step that may endanger his popularity with the Legislature, on his influence over which the figure he is to make will depend." In conclusion, Morris "considered an election by the people as the best, by the Legislature as the worst, mode. Putting both of these aside, he could not but favor the idea of Mr. Wilson, of introducing a mixture of lot."[83] Morris was here referring to James Wilson's proposal on July 24 that the national executive be chosen by a small number, not more than fifteen, of the national legislature, to be drawn from it not by ballot, but by lot, and who should retire immediately and make the election without separating. Wilson said that this mode would avoid intrigue, but "[t]his was not ... a digested idea and might be liable to strong objections."[84]

Hugh Williamson of North Carolina "was sensible that strong objections lay agst. an election of the Executive by the Legislature, and that it opened a door for foreign influence. The principal objection agst. an election by the people seemed to be, the disadvantage under which it would place the smaller States." He suggested as a cure for this difficulty that each voter should vote for three candidates. One of these, he observed, would be probably of his own state, the other two of some other states, and as probably of a small as a large one. Gouverneur Morris "liked the idea, suggesting as an amendment that each man should vote for two persons one of whom at least should not be of his own state."[85] This idea eventually made its way into Article II, Section 1, Clause 3 of the original Constitution in the context of a different procedure: "The Electors [appointed in such manner as the state legislatures, respectively, direct] shall meet in their respective States, and vote by Ballot for two persons, of whom one at least shall not be an Inhabitant of the same State with themselves." As discussed in Chapter 3 of this book, this provision was superseded by the Twelfth Amendment, which was ratified on June 15, 1804.

James Madison now weighed in, saying that something valuable might be made of Williamson's suggestion with Morris's amendment. A person from a small state would likely vote for someone from his state, as his first choice, and a more generally known person from another state as his second. Aggregating the votes from all the states would probably result in "the second best man" being the "first, in fact." As for the objection that the voter would throw away his second vote in order to help his first choice, "it could hardly be supposed that the Citizens of many States would be so sanguine of having their favorite elected, as not to give their second vote with sincerity to the next object of their choice. It might moreover be provided in favor of the smaller States that the Executive should not be eligible more than [number left blank] times in [number left blank] years from the same State."[86] The irony of the last statement is seen in the historical fact that of the first five presidents (Washington, Adams, Jefferson, Madison, and Monroe), only John Adams was not a Virginian.

The remarks of several delegates in favor of a popular election of the national executive provoked the ire of Elbridge Gerry: "A popular election in this case is radically vicious. The ignorance of the people would put it in the power of some one set of men dispersed through the Union & acting in Concert to delude them into any appointment. He observed that such a Society of men existed in the Order of the Cincinnati. . . . They will in fact elect the chief Magistrate in every instance, if the election be referred to the people."[87] Note: The Society of the Cincinnati consisted of certain officers of the United States in the Revolutionary War and their descendants. Originally, membership was hereditary. There was much controversy about the Cincinnati organization at the time of the meeting of the Constitutional Convention, with many taking the position that it was the nucleus of a permanent, hereditary aristocracy.[88]

John Dickinson of Delaware stated that the discussion thus far had demonstrated "insuperable objections" against an election of the executive by either the national legislature or by the legislatures or executives of the states. **"He had long leaned towards an election by the people which he regarded as the best and purest source."** He ascertained that the greatest difficulty of popular election "seemed to arise from the partiality of the States to their respective Citizens. But, might not this very partiality be turned to a useful purpose[?] Let the people of each State chuse its best Citizen. The people will know the most eminent characters of their own States, and the people of the different States will feel an emulation in selecting those of which they will have the greatest reason to be proud— Out of the thirteen names thus selected, an Executive Magistrate may be chosen either by the Natl Legislature, or by Electors appointed by it."[89]

The Convention then voted against postponing Charles Pinckney's motion in order to make way for some such proposition as had been hinted by Hugh Williamson and others. The Convention also rejected Pinckney's motion for a rotation of office of the national executive. Both votes were five votes in favor and six states against, with ten of the eleven voting states voting differently on these two questions.[90]

July 26

George Mason gave an extended speech in which he reviewed the discussion of the various possible methods of selecting the executive. "After reviewing all these various modes, he was led to conclude—that an election by the Natl Legislature as originally proposed, was the best. If it was liable to objections, it was liable to fewer than any other. He conceived at the same time that a second election [election to a second term] ought to be absolutely prohibited." Accordingly, "He concluded with moving that the constitution of the Executive as reported by the Come. [Committee] of the whole be re-instated, viz. 'that the Executive be appointed for seven years, & be ineligible a 2d. time.'" The Convention voted seven states to three in favor of this resolution. Connecticut, Pennsylvania, and Delaware voted no.[91]

The Convention next considered the entire resolution respecting the supreme executive, which read as follows: "Resolved That a national Executive be instituted[,] to consist of a Single Person[,] to be chosen by the national Legislature for the term of seven years[,] to be ineligible a second time[,] with power to carry into execution the national Laws[,] to appoint to Offices in cases not otherwise provided for[,] to be removable on impeachment and conviction of malpractice or neglect of duty[,] to receive a fixed compensation for the devotion of his time to public service to be paid out of the public Treasury." Six states (New Hampshire, Connecticut, North Carolina, South Carolina, and Georgia) voted in favor of this resolution, three states (Pennsylvania, Delaware, and Maryland) voted against, and one state (Virginia) was divided. Massachusetts and New York were absent, and Rhode Island, of course, was never present at the Convention. Madison explained in his notes that Massachusetts "was not on floor . . . ." With regard to the tie in the Virginia vote, Madison stated that John Blair and George Mason voted aye, George Washington and James Madison voted no, and Edmund Randolph "happened to be out of the House."[92]

After discussion of other matters, the Convention unanimously agreed to refer such proceedings as had been agreed on since Monday, July 23, to the Committee of Detail, and it then adjourned until Monday, August 6, to give the Committee of Detail time, in Madison's words, "to prepare & report the Constitution."[93]

August 6

The Committee of Detail submitted its report to the Convention. This included a draft constitution that contained the language of many provisions that ultimately made their way into the final Constitution. Here we see the terms "President," "House of Representatives," and

"Senate"—terms that were more frequently used by the delegates after this point in the Convention. Although the term "Congress" was also in this Committee's report, the delegates continued to use the term "Legislature," perhaps to avoid confusion with the existing Confederation Congress. [94]

Article X (misnumbered "IX"), Section 1 of this draft read as follows: "The Executive Power of the United States shall be vested in a single person. His stile shall be 'The President of the United States of America;' and his title shall be 'His Excellency'. [The title "His Excellency" was later dropped.] He shall be elected by ballot by the Legislature. He shall hold his office during the term of seven years; but shall not be elected a second time"[95]

South Carolina delegate John Rutledge, on behalf of the Committee of Detail, read the draft constitution to the delegates, and each delegate received a printed copy. Thereafter the Convention adjourned to the following day at 11:00 a.m. to give the delegates some time to study the document.[96]

August 7

The delegates briefly discussed whether to have a joint ballot of both houses of Congress when selecting the president, but most of the debate on this day was over other provisions in the draft constitution.[97]

Madison's Notes after August 21: Bilder's Unconformity Theory

Professor Mary Sarah Bilder argues that Madison's Convention notes after August 21 were prepared not during the Convention but rather more than two years later:

> The notes were never finished during the Convention in 1787. Following August 21, there is, to borrow a geological term, an unconformity—a missing section of time. Madison composed the Notes for the remainder of the Convention after the fall of 1789. His comments in these final weeks are thus particularly unreliable. He appears to have continued to take rough notes but had later difficulties in deciphering them. If Madison gave lengthy speeches, he kept no record. Throughout the Convention, the Notes had been necessarily written in hindsight. But the Notes for the final weeks of the Convention were drafted with the advantages of a distance of two years—an entirely different vantage point.[98]

Bilder suggests that this break in Madison's notes was caused by some important developments. From this point on, Madison was heavily involved in committee work and in drafting the final Constitution. "On Wednesday, August 22, Madison was chosen as a member of an important committee. He also became sick. The combination led to the initial collapse of the Notes."[99]

Bilder's conclusion may, however, be questioned in light of the following considerations. Many of Madison's post-August 21 notes are long, detailed, and complicated. It is unlikely that he first prepared this complex material more than two years later from rough notes taken during the Convention proceedings. Perhaps he initially prepared drafts of the post-August 21 notes (utilizing the rough notes and his recollections) either at the time of the Convention or shortly thereafter. Bilder's argument depends, in part, on her observation of the different paper used for the post-August 21 notes.[100] But Madison may have initially written drafts of daily proceedings (utilizing, in part, his rough notes) on the same paper with which he prepared the earlier notes and then later prepared a second draft on different paper, while discarding both the first draft and the rough notes when the second draft was completed. (I am not considering the "rough notes" as a draft of the notes but rather as a source of the first drafts.) Since we know that time was in short supply for Madison during the final weeks of the Convention, perhaps the first drafts of the daily proceedings (prepared from his rough notes and recollections during or shortly after the Convention) were too messy for preservation, so he later prepared a more polished second draft, utilizing the later paper on which we find that later draft. Again, after Madison prepared the second draft, he may have discarded both the rough notes and the first draft. The second draft undoubtedly also contained some revisions of the first draft, which would account for Bilder's observations regarding stylistic conventions:

> The style of the Notes in the post-August 21 section differs from the earlier Notes. Madison wrote his name out in full, "Madison," instead of his usual practice of "M" or leaving a blank. The ubiquitous 'Elseworth' of the early notes became 'Elsworth.' Madison also made relatively few corrections to the text.[101]

It is probable that Madison made some revisions to his hastily written first drafts when he prepared the second draft. If the extant notes are a later revision of first drafts that were prepared during or soon after the Convention, it would make sense that Madison would use the stylistic conventions he employed at the later time. Moreover, the fact that "Madison also made relatively few corrections to the text" is perfectly consistent with the hypothesis that the text we have is itself a revised version of earlier, less polished drafts written in haste during the hectic last few weeks of the Convention.

We shall probably never have a definitive answer regarding these questions. Bilder's views should, however, be kept in mind as the post-August 21 notes are perused, whether or not one ultimately agrees with her.

August 24

The Convention took up Article X, Section 1 of the draft constitution that had been proposed by the Committee of

Detail on August 6: "The Executive Power of the United States shall be vested in a single person. His stile shall be 'The President of the U[nited] S[tates] of America;' and his title shall be 'His Excellency'. He shall be elected by ballot by the Legislature. He shall hold his office during the term of seven years; but shall not be elected a second time."[102]

The Convention first considered the proposition that "The Executive Power of the United States shall be vested in a single person." This proposition passed *nem. con* (without dissent or objection).[103] This development was a significant change from the Articles of Confederation and most state governments, which had weak and/or plural executives.

The Convention also approved, *nem. con*, the next sentence of the section: "His stile shall be 'The President of the U[nited] S[tates] of America;' and his title shall be 'His Excellency'."[104] The title "His Excellency" was later dropped.

The remaining sentences in Section 1 were, however, quite controversial: "He shall be elected by ballot by the Legislature. He shall hold his office during the term of seven years; but shall not be elected a second time."

The first flare-up was a continuation of the discussion on August 7. John Rutledge of South Carolina moved to insert "joint" before the word "ballot." He considered this "the most convenient mode of electing."[105]

Roger Sherman of Connecticut objected to a joint ballot "as depriving the *States* represented in the *Senate* of the negative intended them in that house."[106]

Nathaniel Gorham of Massachusetts "said it was wrong to be considering, at every turn whom the Senate would represent. The public good was the true object to be kept in view— Great delay and confusion would ensue if the two Houses shd vote separately, each having a negative on the choice of the other."[107]

Once again, the clash between small states (Sherman for New Jersey) and large states (Gorham for Massachusetts) had reared its ugly head. Sherman was also arguing for the rights of states as such, whereas Gorham was arguing for the "public good." This kind of conflict was to continue, both in the present discussion and, later, when the procedures for selecting a president were in the final stages of debate.

Jonathan Dayton, another New Jersey delegate, responded to Gorham by observing that it might be well for those who wished to keep the Senate out of sight not to consider how the Senate was constituted. But "a *joint* ballot would in fact give the appointment to one House [the House of Representatives]. He said he could never agree to a joint ballot. He thought that the two houses would separately concur in the same person for president, because "[t]he importance & necessity of the case would ensure <a concurrence>."[108]

At this juncture a surprising thing happened. Daniel Carroll of Maryland suddenly moved to strike out "by the legislature" and insert "by the people" so that the provision would read that the president "shall be elected by ballot by the people." James Wilson of Pennsylvania seconded the motion. However, the motion failed, with nine states voting against it and only two states (Pennsylvania and Delaware) voting for it.[109]

Resuming the debate about inserting the word "joint" before the word "ballot" in the Committee of Detail's draft, David Brearly of New Jersey expressed opposition to that motion.[110]

James Wilson "urged the reasonableness of giving the larger States a larger share of the appointment, and the danger of delay from a disagreement of the two Houses."[111]

John Langdon of New Hampshire supported the motion to elect the president by the joint ballot of the Senate and House of Representatives. He observed that the mode of separate votes by two houses of the bicameral legislature in New Hampshire "was productive of great difficulties." He was in favor of a joint ballot "tho' unfavorable to N. Hampshire as a small State."[112]

James Madison stated: "If the amendment [for a joint ballot] be agreed to[,] the rule of voting will give to the largest State, compared with the smallest, an influence of 4 to 1 only, altho' the population is as 10 to 1. This surely cannot be unreasonable as the President is to act for the *people* not for the *States*."[113]

The Convention then voted in favor of inserting "joint" before "ballot," thus amending the provision to read that the president "shall be elected by joint ballot by the [national] Legislature." Seven states voted aye; four voted no.[114]

Jonathan Dayton then moved to insert after the word "Legislature" the words "each State having one vote."

David Brearly seconded the motion, but it was defeated by five ayes to six noes.[115]

Charles Pinckney moved to insert after the word "Legislature" the words "to which election a majority of the votes of the members present shall be required." This motion was approved by ten ayes to one no. New Jersey was the sole dissenter.[116]

George Read of Delaware "moved 'that in case the numbers for the two highest in votes should be equal, then the President of the Senate shall have an additional casting vote,' which was disagreed to by a general negative."[117]

Gouverneur Morris then gave a long speech opposing the election of the president by the national legislature. In Madison's words,

> He dealt on the danger of rendering the Executive uninterested in maintaining the rights of his Station, as leading to Legislative tyranny. If the Legislature have the Executive dependent on them, they can perpetuate & support their usurpations by the influence of tax-gatherers & other officers, by fleets[,] armies &c. Cabal & corruption are attached to that mode of election: so also is ineligibility a second time. Hence the Executive is interested in Courting popularity in the Legislature by sacrificing his Executive rights; & then he can go into that Body, after the expiration of his Executive Office, and enjoy there the fruits of his policy. To these considerations he added that rivals would be

continually intriguing to oust the President from his place.[118]

To guard against all these evils, Morris moved that the president "shall be chosen by Electors to be chosen by the people of the several States." Daniel Carroll of Maryland seconded the motion, but it was defeated by five ayes (Connecticut, New Jersey, Pennsylvania, Delaware, and Virginia) to six noes (New Hampshire, Massachusetts, Maryland, North Carolina, South Carolina, and Georgia).[119]

After all this discussion and voting, the language of the provision under consideration was as follows: "He [the president] shall be elected by joint ballot by the Legislature, to which election a majority of the votes of the members present shall be required. He shall hold his office during the term of seven years; but shall not be elected a second time."

Jacob Broom of Delaware moved to refer these two clauses (meaning, in this context, sentences) to a Committee of a member from each state, which failed by a vote of five to five with Connecticut being equally divided.[120]

The Convention then considered the first part (the president "shall be chosen by electors") of Gouverneur Morris's previous motion "as an abstract question" (Madison's words), but it was defeated four states to four states with one state (Massachusetts) absent and two states (Connecticut and Maryland) equally divided.[121]

At the request of the New Jersey delegates, the consideration of these provisions for the selection of the president was postponed until the next day (August 25).[122]

August 31

Although the Convention had postponed further consideration of the presidential selection mechanism until August 25, it did not return to that discussion during the remainder of August. Instead, on August 31, on the motion of Roger Sherman, "it was agreed to refer such parts of the Constitution as have been postponed, and such parts of Reports as have not been acted on, to a Committee of a member from each state." James Madison was appointed to this committee for Virginia. The other committee members were Nicholas Gilman (New Hampshire), Rufus King (Massachusetts), Roger Sherman (Connecticut), David Brearly (New Jersey), Gouverneur Morris (Pennsylvania), John Dickinson (Delaware), Daniel Carroll (Maryland), Hugh Williamson (North Carolina), Pierce Butler (South Carolina), and Abraham Baldwin (Georgia).[123]

September 4

The Committee of Eleven appointed on August 31 reported its proposed language regarding the office of the president on September 4.[124] The result seems shocking at first glance but perhaps not so much considering the August 24 tie vote (four to four with Massachusetts being absent and Connecticut and Maryland being equally divided) on the "abstract question" of whether the president "shall be chosen by electors." It should be noted that Gouverneur Morris's earlier resolution that day, providing that the president "shall be chosen by Electors to be chosen by the people of the several States," had been defeated by six noes to five ayes. Accordingly, the Committee may have thought that a system of electors chosen by procedures determined by the state legislatures had a better chance of being approved by the Convention. Additionally, those delegates who had been disturbed by the procedure of a "joint ballot" of the national legislature might have reconsidered any loyalty to the notion of the national legislature electing the president. The language before the Convention at the end of its August 24 session was as follows: "He [the president] shall be elected by joint ballot by the Legislature, to which election a majority of the votes of the members present shall be required. He shall hold his office during the term of seven years; but shall not be elected a second time." Although the Convention had voted on parts of these two sentences, it had not voted on the entire provision. The draft constitutional language of the present Committee of Eleven (which included both James Madison and Gouverneur Morris) replaced those sentences with the following:

> He [the President] shall hold his office during the term of four years, and together with the Vice President, chosen for the same term, be elected in the following manner.

Each State shall appoint in such manner as it's [*sic*] Legislature may direct, a number of Electors equal to the whole number of Senators, and Members of the House of Representatives to which the State may be entitled in the [national] legislature.

The Electors shall meet in their respective States, and vote by ballot for two Persons, of whom one at least shall not be an inhabitant of the same State with themselves. — and shall make a list of all the Persons voted for, and of the number of votes for each, which list they shall sign and certify, and transmit sealed to the seat of the general Government, directed to the President of the Senate.

The President of the Senate shall in that House open all the certificates, and the votes shall be then and there counted — The Person having the greatest number of votes shall be the President, if such number be a majority of the Electors and if there be more than One, who have such Majority, and have an equal number of votes, then the Senate shall choose by ballot one of them for President: but if no Person have a majority, then from the five highest on the list, the Senate shall choose by ballot one of them for President — and in every case after the choice of the President, the Person having the greatest number of votes shall be Vice President: but if there should remain two or more, who have equal votes, the Senate shall choose from them the Vice President.

The [national] Legislature may determine the time of choosing and assembling the Electors, and the manner of certifying and transmitting their votes.[125]

John Dickinson later claimed that the change in the Committee of Eleven from selection of the president by the national legislature to electors appointed in such manner as the state legislatures would direct was instigated by himself with James Madison as the scrivener.[126]

The Convention then discussed the above-quoted language of the Committee. Nathaniel Gorham of Massachusetts "disapproved of making the next highest after the President, the vice-President, without referring the decision to the Senate in case the next highest should have less than a majority of votes. [A]s the regulation stands[,] a very obscure man with very few votes may arrive at that appointment."[127]

Connecticut delegate Roger Sherman, who was a member of the Committee, stated that "the object of this clause of the report of the Committee was to get rid of the ineligibility, which was attached to the mode of election by the [national] Legislature." He continued: "As the choice of the President was to be made out of the five highest [candidates], obscure characters were sufficiently guarded against in that case: And he had no objection to requiring the vice-President to be chosen in like manner, where the choice was not decided by a majority in the first instance."[128]

James Madison then gave a speech on this subject, which he summarized in his notes as follows:

> Mr. Madison was apprehensive that by requiring both the President & vice President to be chosen out of the five highest candidates, the attention of the electors would be turned too much to making candidates instead of giving their votes in order to a definitive choice. Should this turn be given to the business, the election would in fact be consigned to the Senate altogether. It would have the effect at the same time, he observed, of giving the nomination of the candidates to the largest States.[129]

Pennsylvania delegate Gouverneur Morris "concurred in, & enforced the remarks of Mr. Madison."[130]

Edmund Randolph (Virginia) and Charles Pinckney (South Carolina) "wished for a particular explanation & discussion of the reasons for changing the mode of electing the Executive."[131]

Pennsylvania delegate Gouverneur Morris, a member of the Committee, then gave an extended speech that Madison summarized as follows:

> Mr. Govr. Morris said he would give the reasons of the Committee and his own. The 1st was the

danger of intrigue & faction if the appointmt. should be made by the [national] Legislature. 2[.] the inconveniency of an ineligibility required by that mode in order to lessen its evils. 3[.] The difficulty of establishing a Court of Impeachments, other than the Senate which would not be so proper for the trial nor the other branch for the impeachment of the President, if appointed by the Legislature. 4. No body had appeared to be satisfied with an appointment by the Legislature. 5. **Many were anxious even for an immediate choice by the people**— 6[.] **— the indispensable necessity of making the Executive independent of the Legislature. — As the Electors would vote at the same time throughout the U.S. and at so great a distance from each other, the great evil of cabal was avoided. It would be impossible also to corrupt them.**[132]

George Mason (Virginia) "confessed that the plan of the Committee had removed some capital objections, particularly the danger of cabal and corruption. It was liable however to this strong objection, that nineteen times in twenty the President would be chosen by the Senate, an improper body for the purpose."[133]

Pierce Butler (South Carolina) "thought the mode not free from objections, but much more [free from objections] than an election by the Legislature, where as in elective monarchies, cabal[,] faction[,] & violence would be sure to prevail."[134]

Charles Pinckney (South Carolina) "stated as objections to the mode[:] 1. that it threw the whole appointment in fact into the hands of the Senate. 2[.] — The Electors will be strangers to the several candidates and of course unable to decide on their comparative merits. 3. It makes the Executive reeligible which will endanger the public liberty. 4. It makes the same body of men which will in fact elect the President his judges in case of an impeachment."[135]

Hugh Williamson (North Carolina) "had great doubts whether the advantage of reeligibility would balance the objection to such a dependence of the President on the Senate for his reappointment. He thought at least the Senate ought to be restrained to the *two* highest on the list.[136]

Gouverneur Morris "said the principal advantage aimed at was that of taking away the opportunity for cabal. The President may be made if thought necessary ineligible on this as well as on any other mode of election. Other inconveniences may be no less redressed on this plan than any other."[137]

Georgia delegate Abraham Baldwin "thought the plan not so objectionable when well considered, as at first view. The increasing intercourse among the people of the States, would render important characters less & less unknown; and the Senate would consequently be less & less likely to have the eventual appointment thrown into their hands."[138]

James Wilson (Pennsylvania) then gave a long speech, which Madison summarized as follows:

> Mr. Wilson. **This subject has greatly divided the House, and will also divide people out of doors. It is in truth the most difficult of all on which we have had to decide. He had never made up an opinion on it entirely to his own satisfaction.** He thought the plan on the whole a valuable improvement on the former. It gets rid of one evil, that of cabal & corruption; & Continental Characters will multiply as we more & more coalesce, so as to enable the electors in every part of the Union to know & judge of them. It clears the way also for a discussion of the question of re-eligibility on its own merits, which the former mode of election seemed to forbid. He thought it might be better however to refer the eventual appointment to the Legislature than to the Senate, and to confine it to a smaller number than five of the Candidates. The eventual election by the Legislature wd. not open cabal anew, as it would be restrained to certain designated objects of choice, and as these must have had the previous sanction of a number of the States: and if the election be made as it ought as soon as the votes of the electors are opened & it is known that no one has a majority of the whole, there can be little danger of corruption— Another reason for preferring the

Legislature to the Senate in this business, was that the House of Reps. will be so often changed as to be free from the influence & faction to which the permanence of the Senate may subject that branch.[139]

Virginia Governor Edmund Randolph "preferred the former mode of constituting the Executive, but if the change was to be made, he wished to know why the eventual election was referred to the *Senate* and not to the *Legislature*? He saw no necessity for this and many objections to it. He was apprehensive also that the advantage of the eventual appointment would fall into the hands of the States near the Seat of Government.[140]

Gouverneur Morris "said the *Senate* was preferred because fewer could then, say to the President, you owe your appointment to us. He thought the President would not depend so much on the Senate for his re-appointment as on his general good conduct."[141]

No further discussion of the selection of the president and vice president occurred on September 4.

September 5

Charles Pinckney renewed his opposition to the procedure recommended by the Committee of Eleven for the appointment of the executive, arguing, first, that "the electors will not have sufficient knowledge of the fittest men, & will be swayed by an attachment to the eminent men of their respective States." Second, "the dispersion of the votes would leave the appointment with the Senate, and as the President's reappointment will thus depend on the Senate he will be the mere creature of that body." Third, the president "will combine with the Senate agst the House of Representatives." Fourth, "[t]his change in the mode of election was meant to get rid of the ineligibility of the President a second time, whereby he will become fixed for life under the auspices of the Senate."[142]

It is interesting to observe that Pinckney, a South Carolina delegate, was evidently not assuaged by the Committee's concession to the South in apportioning electors to each state on the basis of that state's total number of senators and representatives, thereby triggering the three-fifths rule that the South's slaves would be counted on the basis of three-fifths of a person for the purpose of apportioning the number of each state's members in the House of Representatives (see the discussion of the Three-Fifths Compromise in the proceedings for July 12, above). Pinckney had always supported the selection of the president by the national legislature.

Elbridge Gerry (Massachusetts) "did not object to [the Committee of Eleven's] plan of constituting the Executive in itself, but should be governed in his final vote by the powers that may be given to the president."[143]

John Rutledge (South Carolina) "was much opposed to the plan reported by the Committee. It would throw the whole power into the Senate. He was also against a re-eligibility." Rutledge moved to postpone the Committee's report and take up the original plan of appointment by the national legislature. That motion failed by a vote of eight noes to two ayes (North Carolina and South Carolina) with one state (New Hampshire) equally divided.[144]

Although George Mason (Virginia) stated that he had not yet made up his mind about the appointment of the executive by the national legislature, he had the following objections to the mode proposed by the Committee: First, "It puts the appointment in fact into the hands of the Senate, as it will rarely happen that a majority of the whole votes will fall on any one candidate: and as the Existing President will always be one of the 5 highest, his re-appointment will of course depend on the Senate." Second, "Considering the powers of the President & those of the Senate, if a coalition should be established between these two branches, they will be able to subvert the Constitution. — The great objection with him would be removed by depriving the Senate of the eventual election. He accordingly moved to strike out the words 'if such number be a majority of that of the electors.'"[145] In other words, Mason would have permitted a plurality rather than a majority of electoral votes to determine the winner. This would have obviated any need for the Senate (or, later, the House of Representatives) to decide who would be president.

Hugh Williamson (North Carolina) seconded Mason's motion. "He could not agree to making the highest tho' not having a majority of the votes, President, to a reference of the matter to the Senate. Referring the appointment to the

Senate lays a certain foundation for corruption & aristocracy."[146]

Gouverneur Morris "thought the point of less consequence than it was supposed on both sides. It is probable that a majority of the votes will fall on the same man. As each elector is to give two votes, more than ¼ will give a majority. Besides as one vote is to be given to a man out of the State, and as this vote will not be thrown away, ½ the votes will fall on characters eminent & generally known." He added that "if the President shall have given satisfaction, the votes will turn on him of course, and a majority of them will reappoint him, without resort to the Senate. If he should be disliked, all disliking him, would take care to unite their votes so as to ensure his being supplanted."[147]

George Mason then commented that "those who think there is no danger of there not being a majority for the same person in the first instance, ought to give up the point to those who think otherwise."[148]

Roger Sherman of Connecticut, who was on the Committee of Eleven, "reminded the opponents of the new mode proposed that if the Small States had the advantage in the Senate's deciding among the five highest candidates, the Large States would have in fact the nomination of these candidates."[149]

Mason's motion to make a plurality (rather than a majority) of electoral votes sufficient to elect the president was defeated. The Journal states that only one state, North

Carolina voted in favor of the motion. Madison's notes state that both North Carolina and Maryland voted aye.[150]

James Wilson now moved to strike out "Senate" and insert the word "Legislature" (i.e., the national legislature composed of both the Senate and House of Representatives) with regard to the backup procedure if no candidate received a majority of the electors' votes.[151]

James Madison now stated his position on the pending issue. **He "considered it as a primary object to render an eventual resort to any part of the Legislature improbable.** He was apprehensive that the proposed alteration would turn the attention of the large States too much to the appointment of candidates, instead of aiming at an effectual appointment of the officer, as the large States would predominate in the Legislature which would have the final choice out of the Candidates. Whereas **if the Senate in which the small States predominate should have the final choice, the concerted efforts of the large States would be to make the appointment in the first instance conclusive."**[152]

Edmund Randolph registered his disapproval of using the Senate as a fallback in the event a majority of the electoral votes did not elect a president: "We have in some revolutions of this plan made a bold stroke for Monarchy. We are now doing the same for an aristocracy. He dwelt on the tendency of such an influence in the Senate over the election of the President in addition to its other powers, to convert that body into a real & dangerous Aristocracy."[153]

John Dickinson (Delaware) "was in favor of giving the eventual election to the Legislature, instead of the Senate — It was too much influence to be superadded to that body."[154]

Wilson's motion to substitute "legislature" for "Senate" was defeated by seven to three (Pennsylvania, Virginia, and South Carolina) states, with one state (New Hampshire) divided.[155]

Madison (seconded by Williamson) then moved to replace the word "majority" with "one third" so that a candidate receiving at least one-third of the electoral votes would be elected president if that person also had more electoral votes than any other candidate. This would have been a major substitution of plurality rule for majority rule in the selection of the president. The purpose of the motion was to prevent recourse to the legislature (the Senate, in the current version of the text).[156]

Elbridge Gerry "objected that this would put it in the power of three or four States to put in whom they pleased."[157]

Hugh Williamson similarly observed: "There are seven States which do not contain one third of the people — If the Senate are to appoint, less than one sixth of the people will have the power."[158]

On the motion to substitute "one third" for "such majority," nine states voted no. Only Virginia and North Carolina voted aye.[159]

Elbridge Gerry then "suggested that the eventual decision should be made by six Senators and seven Representatives chosen by joint ballot of both Houses."[160]

Rufus King (Massachusetts) "observed that the influence of the Small States in the Senate was somewhat balanced by the influence of the large States in bringing forth the candidates, and also by the Concurrence of the small States in the Committee in the clause vesting the exclusive origination in the clause vesting the exclusive origination of Money bills in the House of Representatives." Madison added here the following footnote in his notes: "This explains the compromise mentioned above by Mr. Govr Morris - Col. Mason Mr Gerry & other members from large States set great value on this privilege of originating money bills. Of this the members from the small States, with some from the large States who wished a high mounted Govt., endeavored to avail themselves, by making that privilege, the price of arrangements in the constitution favorable to the small States, and to the elevation of the Government."[161]

George Mason moved to strike out the word "five" and insert the word "three" as the highest candidates for the Senate to choose out of." Elbridge Gerry seconded the motion.[162]

Roger Sherman stated he "would sooner give up the plan. He would prefer seven or thirteen."[163]

On Mason's motion to substitute "three" for "five" candidates for consideration of the Senate, the vote was two ayes (Virginia and North Carolina) and eight noes.[164]

Richard Spaight (North Carolina), seconded by John Rutledge, moved to strike out "five" and insert "thirteen" as to the number of candidates for consideration of the Senate. All states except North Carolina and South Carolina voted against this motion.[165]

Madison moved, seconded by Williamson, to insert after "Electors" the words "who shall have balloted" so that the nonvoting electors would not be counted in determining what constituted a majority of electoral votes. This motion was defeated by seven noes to four ayes (Pennsylvania, Maryland, Virginia, and North Carolina).[166]

Dickinson moved to add the word "appointed" to the language "if such number be a majority of the whole number of the Electors." This motion was granted, with only Virginia and North Carolina voting against it.[167]

George Mason stated his dismay as to the results of the discussion concerning the appointment of the executive: "As the mode of appointment is now regulated, he could not forbear expressing his opinion that it is utterly inadmissible. He would prefer the Government of Prussia to one which will put all power into the hands of seven or eight men, and fix an Aristocracy worse than absolute monarchy."[168]

Madison concluded his account of this day's proceedings by stating the following: "The words 'and of their giving their votes' being inserted on motion for that purpose, after the words 'The Legislature may determine the time of chusing and assembling the Electors.'"[169]

Madison's notes say nothing else about this development, and the Journal is silent about it.

September 6

Rufus King, seconded by Elbridge Gerry, moved to insert the following language into the draft constitution submitted by the Committee of Eleven: "But no Person shall be appointed an Elector who is a member of the Legislature of the United States or who holds any office of profit or trust under the United States." This passed *nem. con.*[170]

Elbridge Gerry proposed that if a president at the end of his term is not reelected by a majority of the electors, and if no other candidate receives a majority of electoral votes, the eventual election should be made by the national legislature. This, he said, "would relieve the President from his particular dependence on the Senate for his continuance in office."[171]

Rufus King (Massachusetts) "liked the idea, as calculated to satisfy particular members & promote unanimity; & as likely to operate but seldom."[172]

George Read of Delaware "opposed it, remarking that if individual members were to be indulged, alterations would be necessary to satisfy most of them."[173]

Williamson (North Carolina) "espoused it as a reasonable precaution against the undue influence of the Senate."[174]

Roger Sherman (Connecticut) "liked the arrangement as it stood, though he should not be averse to some amendments. . . . [I]f the Legislature were to have the eventual appointment instead of the Senate, it ought to vote in the case by States, in favor of the small States, as the large States would have so great an advantage in nominating the candidates."[175]

Gouverneur Morris (Pennsylvania) "thought favorably of Mr. Gerry's proposition. It would free the President from being tempted in naming to Offices, to Conform to the will of the Senate, & thereby virtually give the appointments to office, to the Senate."[176]

James Wilson (Pennsylvania) said that, after weighing carefully "the report of the Committee for remodelling the constitution of the Executive; and on combining it with other parts of the plan, he was obliged to consider the whole as having a dangerous tendency to aristocracy; as throwing a dangerous power into the hands of the Senate. They will have in fact, the appointment of the President, and through his dependence on them, the virtual appointment to offices; among others the offices of the Judiciary Department. They are to make Treaties; and they are to try all impeachments. In allowing them thus to make the Executive & Judiciary appointments, to be the Court of impeachments, and to make Treaties which are to be laws of the land, the Legislative, Executive, & Judiciary powers are all blended in one branch of the Government. The power of making Treaties involves the case of subsidies, and **here as an additional evil, foreign influence is to be dreaded— According to the plan as it now stands, the President will not be the man of the people as he ought to be, but the Minion of the Senate.** He cannot even appoint a tide-waiter without the Senate. . . . Upon the whole, he thought the new mode of appointing the President, with some amendments, a valuable improvement; but he could never agree to purchase it at the price of the ensuing parts of the Report, nor befriend a system of Which they make a part."[177]

Gouverneur Morris disagreed with Wilson's views, going into detail about how the plan under discussion did not establish an aristocracy in the Senate.[178]

Williamson observed that "[t]he aristocratic complexion proceeds from the change in the mode of appointing the president which makes him dependent on the Senate."[179]

Pennsylvania delegate George Clymer "said that the aristocratic part to which he could never accede was that in the printed plan, which gave the Senate the power of appointing to Offices."[180]

Alexander Hamilton, who had been absent from the Convention during considerable periods of time and who rarely spoke on the floor, now gave a speech in which he said that "he had been restrained from entering into the discussions by his dislike of the Scheme of Govt in General; but as he meant to support the plan to be recommended, as better than nothing, he wished in this place to offer a few remarks. He liked the new modification, on the whole, better than that in the printed Report." In the former printed report, "the president was a Monster elected for seven years, and ineligible afterwards; having great powers, in appointments to office, &

continually tempted by this constitutional disqualification to abuse them in order to subvert the Government — Although he should be made re-eligible, Still if appointed by the Legislature, he would be tempted to make use of corrupt influence to be continued in office — It seemed peculiarly desirable therefore that Some other mode of election should be devised. Considering the different views of different States & the different districts Northern Middle & Southern, he concurred with those who thought that the votes would not be concentered, and that the appointment would consequently in the present mode devolve on the Senate." He thought that the "nomination to offices will give great weight to the President — Here then is a mutual connection & influence, that will perpetuate the President and aggrandize both him & the Senate. What is to be the remedy? He saw none better than to let the highest number of ballots, whether a majority or not, appoint the President. What was the objection to this? Merely that too small a number might appoint. But as the plan stands, the Senate may take the candidate having the smallest number of votes and make him President."[181] Maryland delegate James McHenry, in his separate notes, recorded Hamilton as saying that he did "not agree with those persons who say they will vote against the report because they cannot get all parts of it to please them — He will take any system which promises to save America from the dangers with which she is threatened."[182]

Motions to extend the president's term from four to seven or six years were defeated, and all states except North Carolina approved a four-year term.[183]

The Convention then approved the following language of the Committee report by nine ayes to two nays (North Carolina and South Carolina): "Each State shall appoint in such manner as it's [*sic*] Legislature may direct, a number of Electors equal to the whole number of Senators, and Members of the House of Representatives to which the State may be entitled in the [national] legislature."[184]

On this date, a number of technical amendments to the Committee's draft constitution were discussed and voted on. In addition, the Journal as well as Madison's notes are unclear with regard to some items. We shall address here only the amendments clearly proposed on this date that were significant.

Spaight said "that if the election by Electors is to be crammed down, he would prefer their meeting altogether and deciding finally without any reference to the Senate." He accordingly moved "That the Electors meet at the seat of the General Government." Williamson seconded this motion, but it was denied, with only North Carolina voting for it.[185] As appears elsewhere in this constitutional history, most delegates considered it important that the electors be dispersed in their separate states in order to avoid undue influence by domestic or foreign actors.

The Convention approved a motion for language requiring the electors to vote on the same day throughout the United States.[186] This again was for the purpose of avoiding undue influence, as they would be separately meeting in their states on the same day, thereby making it more difficult for domestic or foreign actors to influence them.

One of the most important issues addressed that day involved the following exchanges and votes.

Williamson "suggested as better than an eventual choice by the Senate, that this choice should be made by the Legislature, voting by *States* and not *per capita.*[187]

Sherman suggested that the House of Representatives would be preferable to the national legislature. He moved to strike out the words "The Senate shall immediately choose . . . " and insert "The House of Representatives shall immediately choose by ballot one of [the top five candidates after the failure of the electoral vote] for President, the members from each State having one vote." Mason "liked the latter mode best as lessening the aristocratic influence of the Senate." Sherman's motion was approved by ten ayes to one no (Delaware).[188] Thus was born a provision of the Constitution that remains in that document today, though the surrounding context is somewhat different as a result of the Twelfth Amendment.

September 8

On this date, with most of the provisions of the Constitution decided, the Convention appointed a Committee of Style to produce a finished document based on the votes heretofore made by the Convention. The following delegates were appointed by ballot to constitute the Committee: William Samuel Johnson (Connecticut), Alexander Hamilton (New York), Gouverneur Morris (Pennsylvania), James Madison (Virginia), and Rufus King (Massachusetts).[189]

September 12

The Committee of Style presented its report to the Convention on this date, and copies were ordered printed for the use of the delegates.[190]

September 15

After some additional amendments not affecting the selection of the president, all of the eleven state delegations present at the Convention (Rhode Island and New York not being present) voted to approve the Constitution, as amended, and the Constitution was ordered to be engrossed.[191] ("From around 1300, when the English language was taking its modern form, up to the 1790s, engrossing was a special large handwriting used for formal legal documents." This practice was, for the framers, anachronistic, since they had used a printer to print various earlier drafts of the Constitution, and printed copies were also made of the final version for public distribution.)[192]

September 17

The Constitution was signed by all delegates present, except for Edmund Randolph, George Mason, and Elbridge Gerry, who declined giving it the sanction of their names.

The Convention then dissolved itself by an adjournment sine die.[193]

Final Text of the 1787 Constitution Regarding the Selection of the President and Vice President

The final text of the provisions on selection of the president and vice president in the 1787 Constitution, as submitted to the state conventions for ratification, was as follows:

Article II

Section 1

1. The executive Power shall be vested in a President of the United States of America. He shall hold his Office during the Term of four Years, and, together with the Vice President, chosen for the same Term, be elected, as follows:

2. Each State shall appoint, in such Manner as the Legislature thereof may direct, a Number of Electors, equal to the whole Number of Senators and Representatives to which the State may be entitled in the Congress: but no Senator or Representative, or Person holding an Office of Trust or Profit under the United States, shall be appointed an Elector.

3. The Electors shall meet in their respective States, and vote by Ballot for two Persons, of whom one at least shall not be an Inhabitant of

the same State with themselves. And they shall make a List of all the Persons voted for, and of the Number of Votes for each; which List they shall sign and certify, and transmit sealed to the Seat of the Government of the United States, directed to the President of the Senate. The President of the Senate shall, in the Presence of the Senate and House of Representatives, open all the Certificates, and the Votes shall then be counted. The Person having the greatest Number of Votes shall be the President, if such Number be a Majority of the whole Number of Electors appointed; and if there be more than one who have such Majority, and have an equal Number of Votes, then the House of Representatives shall immediately chuse by Ballot one of them for President; and if no Person have a Majority, then from the five highest on the List the said House shall in like Manner chuse the President. But in chusing the President, the Votes shall be taken by States, the Representation from each State having one Vote; A quorum for this Purpose shall consist of a Member or Members from two thirds of the States, and a Majority of all the States shall be necessary to a Choice. In every Case, after the Choice of the President, the Person having the greatest Number of Votes of the Electors shall be the Vice President. But if there should remain two or more who have equal Votes, the Senate shall chuse from them by Ballot the Vice President.

4. The Congress may determine the Time of chusing the Electors, and the Day on which they shall give their Votes; which Day shall be the same throughout the United States.[194]

The entire 1787 Constitution (including these provisions) was ratified by the requisite number of states on June 21, 1788. The first and second clauses quoted above remain in effect as of the time of this writing. The entirety of the third clause set forth above was superseded by the Twelfth Amendment (ratified June 15, 1804).

NOTES

1. The Intentions of the Framers of the Electoral College

[1] This book's principal source for the delegates' notes and other records pertaining to the Constitutional Convention is Max Farrand, ed., *The Records of the Federal Convention of 1787*, 4 vols. (New Haven, CT: Yale University Press, 1966). See note 1 of the Appendix to the present book for a more complete discussion of these records and the use of them in this book. See also the section "Madison's Notes after August 21: Bilder's Unconformity Theory," which is located after the entry for August 7 in the Appendix.

[2] Farrand, *Records*, 2:501 (Madison's notes).

[3] Merrill Jensen, *The Articles of Confederation: An Interpretation of the Social-Constitutional History of the American Revolution, 1774-1781* (1940; repr., Madison: University of Wisconsin Press, 1966), 238.

[4] Andrew C. McLaughlin, *The Confederation and the Constitution, 1783-1789* (New York: Collier Books, 1962), 46-47; Richard B. Morris, *The Forging of the Union, 1781-1789* (New York: Harper & Row, 1987), 99 (quotation); Pauline Maier, *Ratification: The People Debate the Constitution, 1787-1788* (New York: Simon & Schuster, 2011), 33.

[5] Farrand, *Records*, 3:13-14 (emphasis added).

[6] Farrand, 1:8 (Journal), 11, 69 (Madison's notes).

[7] Farrand, 1:xix.

[8] Farrand, 1:69 (Madison's notes).

[9] Farrand, 2:106 (Madison's notes). For a good, brief account of James Wilson's political views, career, and tragic end, see Christopher Collier and James Lincoln Collier, *Decision in Philadelphia: The Constitutional Convention of 1787* (New York: Ballantine Books, 1986), 279-88. See also the following full-length biography: Charles Page Smith, *James Wilson, Founding Father, 1742-1798* (Chapel Hill, NC: University of North Carolina Press, 1956).

[10] Farrand, *Records*, 2:29 (Madison's notes).

[11] Willi Paul Adams, *The First American Constitutions: Republican Ideology and the Making of the State Constitutions in the Revolutionary Era*, expanded ed., trans. Rita and Robert Kimber (Lanham, MD: Madison House, 2001), 294.

[12] Allan Nevins, *The American States During and After the Revolution, 1775-1789* (1924; repr., New York: Augustus M. Kelley, 1969), 4, 164; Adams, *The First American Constitutions*, 64.

[13] Farrand, *Records*, 2:52 (Madison's notes).

[14] Farrand, 2:55-56 (Madison's notes).

[15] Farrand, 2:30 (Madison's notes). With regard to blank paper ballots, an eminent American historian has noted that "few states used printed ballots at this time [the 1790s]. Voters were often simply given a blank sheet of paper and told to write their choice of candidates." John Ferling, *Adams*

vs. Jefferson: The Tumultuous Election of 1800 (New York: Oxford University Press, 2004), 86.

[16] Farrand, *Records*, 2:56-57 (Madison's notes) (emphasis added).

[17] Farrand, 2:111 (Madison's notes) (emphasis added).

[18] Adams, *First American Constitutions*, 161, 194-215, 312, 315-327; Nevins, *American States*, 170.

[19] "[S]ingle women owning property 'worth fifty pounds' were allowed to vote in New Jersey between 1776 and 1807 before the right was restricted to white males." Christopher Klein, "The State Where Women Voted Long Before the Nineteenth Amendment," August 26, 2015, *History*, http://www.history.com/news/the-state-where-women-voted-long-before-the-19th-amendment.

[20] Adams, *First American Constitutions*, 161.

[21] Nevins, *American States*, 447-49; Adams, *First American Constitutions*, 180-83.

[22] See the discussion and notes in the Appendix for July 12 and 16. For accounts of how the Three-Fifths Clause may (or may not) have affected presidential elections and legislation in the early republic, see David O. Stewart, *The Summer of 1787: The Men Who Invented the Constitution* (New York: Simon & Schuster, 2007), 261-64, and George William Van Cleve, *A Slaveholders' Union: Slavery, Politics, and the Constitution in the Early American Republic* (Chicago: University of Chicago Press, 2010), 139-142

[23] Farrand, *Records*, 3:25 (May 21, 1787 letter of Delaware delegate George Read to Delaware delegate John Dickinson). Read referred to "a copied draft of a Federal system intended to be proposed, if something nearly similar shall not precede it." Read's letter stated, among other things, that a bicameral legislature was being contemplated, with the first house (what became the House of Representatives) consisting of representatives allocated to each state "in proportion to its number of white inhabitants, and three-fifths of all others."

[24] Farrand, 1:590-91 (Journal), 591-97 (Madison's notes).

[25] Farrand, 2:60-63 (Journal), 64 (Madison's notes).

[26] Farrand, 2:114-15 (Madison's notes).

[27] Farrand, 2:307, 399 (Journal), 2:402 (Madison's notes).

[28] Farrand, 2:57 (Madison's notes).

[29] Farrand, 2:114 (Madison's notes).

[30] Farrand, 2:29 (Madison's notes).

[31] Farrand, 2:30 (Madison's notes).

[32] Farrand, 2:30-31 (Madison's notes).

[33] Farrand, 2:31 (Madison's notes).

[34] Farrand, 2:111 (Madison's notes).

[35] Farrand, 2:112 (Madison's notes).

[36] Farrand, 1:18-23 (Madison's notes), 23-24 (Robert Yates's notes), 24-27 (James McHenry's notes), 27-28 (William Paterson's notes). Yates was a delegate from New York, McHenry from Maryland, and Paterson from New Jersey.

[37] Farrand, 1:21 (Madison's notes).

[38] Morris, *Forging of the Union*, 288 (only four states "allowed eligible voters to elect their governor; in eight he was chosen by the legislature").

[39] Farrand, *Records*, 1:68 (Madison's notes). See also Tadisha Kuroda, *The Origins of the Twelfth Amendment: The Electoral College in the Early Republic, 1787-1804* (Westport, CT: Greenwood, 1994), 8; Richard Beeman, *Plain, Honest Men: The Making of the American Constitution* (New York: Random House, 2010), 27-28, 105-6, 125-28, 230.

[40] Jefferson to Samuel Kercheval, July 12, 1816, *Founders Online*, National Archives, last modified June 29, 2017, http://founders.archives.gov/documents/Jefferson/03-10-02-0128-0002. Jefferson did not capitalize the beginning letter in a sentence except at the beginning of a paragraph. These initial letters of sentences have been capitalized in the quotation for the convenience of the reader.

[41] Farrand, *Records*, 1:20 (Madison's notes).

[42] Farrand, 1:242-44 (Madison's notes); Farrand, 3:611-13 (New Jersey Plan documents).

[43] For additional information and documentation, see the entries for the listed dates in the Appendix.

[44] Farrand, *Records*, 2:97-98 (Journal), 99-101 (Madison's notes). For the July 19 decision for electors appointed by the state legislatures, see Farrand, 2:50-51 (Journal), 57-58 (Madison's notes).

[45] Farrand, 1:80 (Madison's notes).

[46] Farrand, 1:175 (Madison's notes).

[47] Farrand, 1:181 (Yates's notes).

[48] Farrand, 2:109 (Madison's notes).

[49] Farrand, 2:29 (Madison's notes).

[50] Farrand, 2:103-4 (Madison's notes) (emphasis added).

[51] Farrand, 2:29-30 (Madison's notes).

[52] Farrand, 2:32 (Madison's notes).

[53] Farrand, 2:56 (Madison's notes) (italics in the original). Madison made similar remarks about the need for separation of powers on July 17. Farrand, 2:34-35.

[54] Farrand, 2:109 (Madison's notes) (emphasis added).

[55] Farrand, 2:121 (Madison's notes).

[56] Farrand, 2:112 (Madison's notes).

[57] Farrand, 2:113 (Madison's notes).

[58] Farrand, 2:114 (Madison's notes).

[59] Farrand, 1:80 (Madison's notes).

[60] Farrand, 1:80 (Madison's notes).

[61] Farrand, 1:80 (Madison's notes).

[62] Farrand, 1:174-75 (Journal), 175-76 (Madison's notes). This vote was taken in the Committee of the Whole (see the entry for May 30 in the Appendix for this procedure). Although Gerry attempted to revive his proposal in the Convention on July 25, his motion was apparently not seconded and did not proceed to a vote. Farrand, 2:109 (Madison's notes).

[63] Farrand, 2:50-51 (Journal), 57-58 (Madison's notes).

[64] Farrand, 1:81 (Madison's notes).

[65] Farrand, 1:77, 79 (Journal), 81 (Madison's notes). The Journal has New York as being divided (thus yielding seven noes), whereas Madison counts it as a "no" (totaling eight noes). The vote was technically on Wilson's motion to substitute his electoral scheme for the Virginia Plan's proposal of election of the national executive by the national legislature.

[66] Farrand, 1:77, 79 (Journal), 81 (Madison's notes).

[67] Farrand, 1:292 (Madison's notes), 300 (Yates's notes).

[68] Farrand, 2:22, 24 (Journal), 32 (Madison's notes).

[69] See the discussion and documentation in the Appendix for the dates of July 12, 16, and 19.

[70] Farrand, *Records*, 2:50-51 (Journal), 57-59 (Madison's notes).

[71] Farrand, 2:58, 60-62 (Journal), 64 (Madison's notes).

[72] Farrand, 2:60-63 (Journal), 64 (Madison's notes).

[73] Farrand, 2:97-98 (Journal), 99-106 (Madison's notes).

[74] Farrand, 2:110 (Madison's notes).

[75] Farrand, 2:110-11 (Madison's notes).

[76] See the Appendix, and the endnotes thereto, for a more detailed account of these developments.

[77] Farrand, *Records*, 2:116, 118 (Journal), 120-21 (Madison's notes).

[78] Farrand, 2:117-18 (Journal), 121 (Madison's notes).

[79] Farrand, 2:185 (Madison's notes).

[80] Farrand, 2:401 (Madison's notes).

[81] Farrand, 2:401 (Madison's notes).

[82] Farrand, 2:401-2 (Madison's notes) (emphasis in the original).

[83] Farrand, 2:402 (Madison's notes).

[84] Farrand, 2:403 (Madison's notes) (emphasis in the original).

[85] Beeman, *Plain, Honest Men*, 160-64, 184, 189, 200, 202, 204, 206, 218, 223-24.

[86] Farrand, *Records*, 2:397, 399 (Journal), 403 (Madison's notes). Connecticut, New Jersey, Maryland, and Georgia voted no. Farrand, 2:399 (Journal), 403 (Madison's notes).

[87] Farrand, 2:397, 399 (Journal), 403 (Madison's notes).

[88] Farrand, 2:397, 399 (Journal), 404 (Madison's notes).

[89] Farrand, 2:397, 399 (Journal), 104 (Madison's notes). New Jersey, Pennsylvania, Delaware, and Virginia voted in favor of the motion. New Hampshire, North Carolina, South Carolina, and Georgia voted against it.

[90] Farrand, 2:473 (Journal), 481 (Madison's notes).

[91] Farrand, 2:493-94 (Journal), 497-98 (Madison's notes) (emphasis added).

[92] John Dickinson to George Logan, January 16, 1802, ConSource: The Constitutional Sources Project, http://www.consource.org/document/john-dickinson-to-george-logan-1802-1-16/ (italic emphasis as in the original, bold emphasis added); cf. James H. Hutson, ed., *Supplement to Max Farrand's "The Records of the Federal Convention of 1787"* (New Haven, CT: Yale University Press, 1987), 300-301.

[93] For the details of the debate over whether the Senate or the House (voting by states) should handle the contingent election of the president, see the entries for September 4-6 in the Appendix.

[94] Farrand, *Records*, 2:517, 520 (Journal), 525 (Madison's notes).

[95] See the Appendix entries for September 8, 15, and 17 for additional details and documentation.

[96] Farrand, *Records*, 2:657-58. The conventional arabic numbering of the clauses (paragraphs) has been added for ease of reference.

[97] Madison to George Hay, August 23, 1823, *Founders Online*, National Archives, last modified June 29, 2017, https://founders.archives.gov/documents/Madison/04-03-02-0109.

[98] As Madison stated in *Federalist* No. 37, "the convention must have been compelled to sacrifice theoretical propriety to the force of extraneous considerations." Under such circumstances, he continued (the first readers did not know the identity of the author), "Would it be wonderful if under the pressure of all these difficulties, the convention should have been forced into some deviations from that artificial structure and regular symmetry, which an abstract view of the subject might lead an ingenious theorist to bestow on a constitution planned in his closet or in his imagination?" *Federalist* No. 37, [11 January] 1788," *Founders Online*, National Archives, last modified June 29, 2017,

https://founders.archives.gov/documents/Madison/01-10-02-0227. The student of the Convention debates is immediately aware that Madison must have been thinking of himself as the "ingenious theorist." Cf. Rakove, *Original Meanings*, 168-69.

[99] I use the term "nationalist" here in the same sense as historian Irving Brant in his book title *James Madison: The Nationalist, 1780-1787* (Indianapolis: Bobbs-Merrill, 1948). James Madison, George Washington, James Wilson, Gouverneur Morris, Alexander Hamilton, and other like-minded individuals of the founding era stressed the importance of a general government—the "national" government—and emphasized the need to curb the excesses of state governments that had been all-powerful during the Articles of Confederation period. Such founders had no notion of the kind of "nationalism" that was sometimes promoted in the nineteenth, twentieth, and twenty-first centuries. The latter was a much different phenomenon. See, for example, the discussion of the latter-day nationalism in E. J. Dionne Jr., Norman J. Ornstein, and Thomas E. Mann, *One Nation After Trump: A Guide for the Perplexed, the Disillusioned, the Desperate, and the Not-Yet Deported* (New York: St. Martin's Press, 2017), Kindle edition, chapter 8. In contrast, Madison later wrote that, in the Constitutional Convention debates, "the term National as contradistinguished from Federal was not meant to express more than that the powers to be vested in the new Government were to operate as in a National Government directly on the people and not as in the old Confederacy on the States only." Madison to

Nicholas P. Trist, December 1, 1831, *Founders Online*, National Archives, last modified June 29, 2017, http://founders.archives.gov/documents/Madison/99-02-02-2483 (Early Access document, emphasis in the original).

2. The Understandings of the Ratifiers of the Electoral College

[1] Farrand, *Records*, 2:665 (emphasis added).

[2] *Journals of the Continental Congress, 1774-1789*, (Washington D.C.: U.S. Government Printing Office, 1933), 33:549 (September 28, 1787), https://memory.loc.gov/cgi-bin/ampage?collId=lljc&fileName=033/lljc033.db&recNum=166&itemLink=r?ammem/hlaw:@field(DOCID+@lit(jc0334 5)):%230330167&linkText=1 (italics in the original, bold emphasis added).

[3] Farrand, *Records*, 1:122-23 (Madison's notes), 126-27 (Yates's notes), 2:476 (Madison's notes); see also Rakove, *Original Meanings*, chap. 5.

[4] Farrand, *Records*, 2:476 (Madison's notes).

[5] Mary Sarah Bilder, *Madison's Hand: Revising the Constitutional Convention* (Cambridge, MA: Harvard University Press, 2015), 235-36.

[6] Jack N. Rakove, *Original Meanings: Politics and Ideas in the Making of the Constitution* (New York: Vintage Books, 1996), chap. 11 passim.

[7] Madison, Speech in House of Representatives, April 6, 1797, *Founders Online*, National Archives, last modified June

29, 2017, https://founders.archives.gov/documents/Madison/01-16-02-0195.

[8] Madison to Nicholas P. Trist, December 1, 1831, *Founders Online*, National Archives, last modified June 29, 2017, http://founders.archives.gov/documents/Madison/99-02-02-2483 (Early Access document). (emphasis in the original).

[9] "One of the reasons [Madison] was inclined [by 1796] to downplay the role of the framers of the Constitution in Philadelphia was that he had by that time come around to embrace views closer to those of the Antifederalist critics of the Constitution than of extreme nationalists like Hamilton." Beeman, *Plain, Honest Men*, 410. Mary Sarah Bilder has a similar interpretation of Madison's April 6, 1796 speech. Bilder, *Madison's Hand*, 219-220 (noting, *inter alia*, that Madison's speech "attempted to diminish the authority of the Convention. He argued that the more legitimate meaning of the Constitution was to be drawn from the records of the ratifications. Madison knew the paltry extent of these records.").

[10] Bilder has argued that Madison made some substantive modifications in his notes over the decades, apparently for the purpose of concealing his earlier views on various matters. *Madison's Hand*, 198-203, 214-220, 244-46, and passim.

[11] Madison, April 6, 1797 Speech.

[12] Bilder, *Madison's Hand*, 220.

[13] Madison, April 6, 1797 Speech.

[14] See, for example, Rakove, *Original Meanings*, 364: "Whatever clarity [Madison] gained by distinguishing framers from ratifiers was clouded by the difficulty of using the ambiguous [state ratification convention] debates and failed amendments of 1787-88 to offset an express constitutional provision").

[15] Madison to Samuel Johnston, June 21, 1789, *Founders Online*, National Archives, last modified June 29, 2017, http://founders.archives.gov/documents/Jefferson/01-15-02-0221.

[16] *Federalist* Number 37, January 11, 1788," *Founders Online*, National Archives, last modified June 29, 2017, https://founders.archives.gov/documents/Madison/01-10-02-0227. Cf. Rakove, *Original Meanings*, 339-42.

[17] Rakove, *Original Meanings*, 6 (quotation), 7-8, 11.

[18] *DHRC*, 2:566-67, http://rotunda.upress.virginia.edu/founders/RNCN-02-02-02-0003-0002-0019.

[19] *DHRC*, 2:567.

[20] *DHRC*, 2:567.

[21] *DHRC*, 6:1363, http://rotunda.upress.virginia.edu/founders/RNCN-02-06-02-0002-0021-0006 (notes of Theophilus Parsons).

[22] *DHRC*, 7:1813, http://rotunda.upress.virginia.edu/founders/RNCN-02-07-03-0001-0020 (Justus Dwight journal).

[23]   *DHRC,*   6:1457,
http://rotunda.upress.virginia.edu/founders/RNCN-02-06-02-0002-0029-0002.

[24]   *DHRC,*   12:639,
http://rotunda.upress.virginia.edu/founders/RNCN-02-12-02-0003-0007 (italics in the original. bold emphasis added).

[25] Maier, *Ratification*, 256-57.

[26] Maier, 258.   As noted above, Madison himself later mentioned the "abundance of chasms [omissions], and misconceptions of what was said" in the report of the speeches.   Madison, April 6, 1797 speech, https://founders.archives.gov/documents/Madison/01-16-02-0195.

[27]   *DHRC,*   10:1098,
http://rotunda.upress.virginia.edu/founders/RNCN-02-10-02-0002-0009.

[28] See Chapters 3 and 4 passim.

[29] Adams, *First American Constitutions*, 328-31.

[30]   *DHRC,*   10:1365,
http://rotunda.upress.virginia.edu/founders/RNCN-02-10-02-0002-0006 (dashes omitted, one period added).

[31] *DHRC*, 10:1365-66.

[32]   *DHRC,*   10:1371,
http://rotunda.upress.virginia.edu/founders/RNCN-02-10-02-0002-0007 (emphasis added).

[33] *DHRC*, 10:1371-73 (emphasis added).

[34] *DHRC*, 10:1373 (emphasis added).

[35] *DHRC*, 10:1373 (emphasis added).

[36] *DHRC*, 10:1373-74.

[37] *DHRC*, 10:1375-76.

[38] *DHRC*, 10: 1377 (emphasis added).

[39] *DHRC*, 10: 1377.

[40] *DHRC*, 10:1412, http://rotunda.upress.virginia.edu/founders/RNCN-02-10-02-0002-0009 (dashes omitted, emphasis added).

[41] *DHRC*, 10:1376-77.

[42] *DHRC*, 10:1386-1410, http://rotunda.upress.virginia.edu/founders/default.xqy?keys=RNCN-print-02-10-02-0002-0008&printable=yes.

[43] Jonathan Elliot, ed., *The Debates in the Several State Conventions of the Adoption of the Federal Constitution as Recommended by the General Convention at Philadelphia in 1787*, 2nd ed., vol. 4 (Philadelphia: J. B. Lippincott, 1866), 58, 74.

[44] Elliot, 4:105.

[45] Elliot, 4:105, 107, 122.

[46] Elliot, 4:106 (emphasis added).

[47] Maier, *Ratification*, 421-23, 457, 458-59; Bernard Schwartz, *The Great Rights of Mankind: A History of the American Bill of Rights*, expanded ed. (Madison, WI: Madison House, 1992), 186.

[48] *DHRC*, 2:170, http://rotunda.upress.virginia.edu/founders/RNCN-02-02-02-0002-0002-0018.

[49] *DHRC*, 2:170.

[50] Maier, *Ratification*, 80-81.

[51] *DHRC*, 27:126, http://rotunda.upress.virginia.edu/founders/RNCN-02-27-02-0002-0009.

[52] *DHRC*, 27:148, http://rotunda.upress.virginia.edu/founders/RNCN-02-27-02-0002-0010 (emphasis added).

[53] *DHRC*, 19:203 (editorial note), 222 (quotation, emphasis added), http://rotunda.upress.virginia.edu/founders/RNCN-02-19-02-0002-0075.

[54] *DHRC*, 4:395, http://rotunda.upress.virginia.edu/founders/RNCN-02-04-02-0003-0138 (emphasis added).

[55] *DHRC*, 19:407, http://rotunda.upress.virginia.edu/founders/RNCN-02-19-02-0002-0150 (emphasis added).

[56] *DHRC*, 16:281, http://rotunda.upress.virginia.edu/founders/RNCN-03-16-02-0092 (emphasis added).

[57] Maier, *Ratification*, 84-85, 257.

[58] Maier, 258, 327, 408, 458.

[59] *Federalist* No. 68, March 12, 1788, *Founders Online*, National Archives, last modified June 29, 2017, https://founders.archives.gov/documents/Hamilton/01-04-02-0218.

[60] *DHRC*, 19:222.

[61] *Federalist* No. 68.

[62] *Federalist* No. 68 (emphasis added).

[63] *Federalist* No. 68 (italics in the original).

[64] *Federalist* No. 68 (emphasis added).

[65] *Federalist* No. 68 (emphasis added).

[66] *Federalist* No. 77, April 2, 1788, *Founders Online*, National Archives, last modified June 29, 2017, https://founders.archives.gov/documents/Hamilton/01-04-02-0229.

[67] Constitution, Art. II, § 1, cl. 2.

[68] *Federalist* No. 64, in Alexander Hamilton, John Jay, and James Madison, *The Federalist*, Gideon Edition, ed. George W. Carey and James McClellan (1818; repr., Indianapolis: Liberty Fund, 2001), 333 (emphasis added). Jay also applied these considerations to senators, who were selected by the state legislatures in this original version of the Constitution. I have used ellipses in the quotation to skip over the references to senators, as such language is not relevant to the issue of the Electoral College.

[69] *Federalist* No. 10, November 22, 1788, *Founders Online*, National Archives, last modified June 29, 2017, https://founders.archives.gov/documents/Madison/01-10-02-0178 (emphasis added).

[70] Gary Bugh, "Representation in Congressional Efforts to Amend the Presidential Election System," in *Electoral College Reform: Challenges and Possibilities*, ed. Gary Bugh (2010; repr., London: Routledge, 2016), 7.

[71] *Federalist* No. 39, January 16, 1788, *Founders Online*, National Archives, last modified June 29, 2017, https://founders.archives.gov/documents/Madison/01-10-02-0234.

[72] *Federalist* No. 45, January 26, 1788, *Founders Online*, National Archives, last modified June 29, 2017, https://founders.archives.gov/documents/Madison/01-10-02-0254.

3. The Early Frustration of Original Intent and the Adoption of the Twelfth Amendment

[1] Hamilton, Jay, and Madison, *Federalist: Gideon Edition*, 540 (editorial note).

[2] *Journals of the Continental Congress, 1774-1789*, 34:523, https://memory.loc.gov/cgi-bin/ampage?collId=lljc&fileName=034/lljc034.db&recNum=532&itemLink=r%3Fammem%2Fhlaw%3A%40field%28DOCID%2B%40lit%28jc0341%29%29%230340001&linkText=1.

[3] *Annals of Congress (The Debates and Proceedings in the Congress of the United States)*, vol. 1, ed., Joseph Gales Sr. (Washington: Gales & Seaton, 1834), 17, https://memory.loc.gov/cgi-bin/ampage?collId=llac&fileName=001/llac001.db&recNum=11; David P. Currie, *The Constitution in Congress: The Federalist Period, 1789-1801* (Chicago: University of Chicago Press, 1997), 4.

[4] Joseph J. Ellis, *His Excellency: George Washington* (New York: Random House, 2004), Kindle ed., Kindle loc. 3300-3301.

[5] Stanley Elkins and Eric McKitrick, *The Age of Federalism: The Early American Republic, 1788-1800* (New York: Oxford University Press, 1993), 33-34.

[6] Neil R. Peirce and Lawrence D. Longley, *The People's President: The Electoral College in American History and the Direct Vote Alternative*, rev. ed. (New Haven: Yale University Press, 1981), 31-32. The New York situation is discussed at length in Kuroda, *Origins of the Twelfth Amendment*, chap. 4.

[7] *DHRC*, 10:1371n19 (editorial note), http://rotunda.upress.virginia.edu/founders/RNCN-02-10-02-0002-0006.

[8] Kuroda, *Origins of the Twelfth Amendment*, 29-31.

[9] Kuroda, 31.

[10] Kuroda, 34-35; Peirce and Longley, *The People's President*, 248; John R. Koza et al., *Every Vote Equal: A State-Based Plan for Electing the President by National Popular Vote* (Los Altos, CA: National Popular Vote Press, 2013), 71 (§ 2.2.1).

[11] Kuroda, *Origins of the Twelfth Amendment*, 32-34, 36-38; Peirce and Longley, *The People's President*, 248; Koza, *Every Vote Equal*, 70 (§ 2.2.1).

[12] Elkins and McKitrick, *Age of Federalism*, 33; Kuroda, *Origins of the Twelfth Amendment*, 28-29, 31-32, 36.

[13] Kuroda, *Origins of the Twelfth Amendment*, chaps. 3-4 passim; Elkins and McKitrick, *Age of Federalism*, 33.

[14] Peirce and Longley, *The People's President*, 33; Kuroda, *Origins of the Twelfth Amendment*, 33, 34; Ron Chernow, *Alexander Hamilton* (New York: Penguin, 2004), 270-73; John Ferling, *John Adams: A Life* (1992; repr., New York: Owl Books, 1996), 298-99.

[15] Peirce and Longley, *The People's President*, 34, 247-48; Kuroda, *Origins of the Twelfth Amendment*, 54-57.

[16] Kuroda, *Origins of the Twelfth Amendment*, 54; Koza, *Every Vote Equal*, 72 (§ 2.2.1); Peirce and Longley, *The People's President*, 34.

[17] Kuroda, *Origins of the Twelfth Amendment*, 57-61 (first quotation at 61), 177; Peirce and Longley, *The People's President*, 34 (second quotation).

[18] Peirce and Longley, *The People's President*, 34-35; Koza, *Every Vote Equal*, 73, 75-77 (§ 2.2.2); Kuroda, *Origins of the Twelfth Amendment*, 63-65.

[19] Kuroda, *Origins of the Twelfth Amendment*, 65-66; Peirce and Longley, *The People's President*, 35-36; James Roger Sharp, *American Politics in the Early Republic: The New Nation in Crisis* (New Haven: Yale University Press, 1993), 146-49; Chernow, *Hamilton*, 509-16; Elkins and McKitrick, *Age of Federalism*, 523-24; Bernard A. Weisberger, *America Afire: Jefferson, Adams, and the First Contested Election* (New York: Perennial, 2001), 166-67; Ferling, *John Adams*, 324-27, 331-32; Ferling, *Adams vs. Jefferson*, chap. 6 passim.

[20] Peirce and Longley, *The People's President*, 248; Kuroda, *Origins of the Twelfth Amendment*, 66-69; Koza, *Every Vote Equal*, 73, 76-77 (§ 2.2.2). Note: these secondary authorities differ among themselves in some particulars on some specifics of the mode of election, for example, in how they classify Georgia.

[21] Kuroda, *Origins of the Twelfth Amendment*, 67, 69; Koza, *Every Vote Equal*, 77-78 (§ 2.2.2); Peirce and Longley, *The People's President*, 35-36.

[22] Peirce and Longley, *The People's President*, 36 (italics in the original).

[23] Peirce and Longley, 35.

[24] Ferling, *Adams vs. Jefferson*, 99-110.

[25] Ferling, 110-24; Elkins and McKitrick, *Age of Federalism*, 590-93, 694-95, 700-711, 714-15, 719-26; Lance Banning, ed., *Liberty and Order: The First American Party Struggle* (Indianapolis: Liberty Fund, 2004), 231-43; Terri Diane Halperin, *The Alien and Sedition Acts of 1800: Testing the Constitution* (Baltimore, Johns Hopkins Press, 2016), chaps 4-5 passim.

[26] Ferling, *Adams vs. Jefferson*, 132; Elkins and McKitrick, *Age of Federalism*, 728, 732-35, 740; Peirce and Longley, *The People's President*, 37.

[27] Ferling, *Adams vs. Jefferson*, 138-43; Elkins and McKitrick, *Age of Federalism*, 692, 732-43.

[28] Sharp, *American Politics*, 243; Peirce and Longley, *The People's President*, 38, 247, 248; Elkins and McKitrick, *Age*

of Federalism, 741, 905n143. Ferling does not mention Tennessee's mixed system, instead counting it as one of eleven states in which the legislature made the decision. *Adams vs. Jefferson*, 156. In contrast, Weisberger claims that Tennessee used a popular vote method of choosing electors in 1800. *America Afire*, 229-30.

[29] Ferling, *Adams vs. Jefferson*, 166 (emphasis added).

[30] Ferling, chap. 12; Kuroda, *Origins of the Twelfth Amendment*, chap. 9; Sharp, *American Politics*, chap. 12; Peirce and Longley, *The People's President*, 39-41; Susan Dunn, *Jefferson's Second Revolution: The Election Crisis of 1800 and the Triumph of Republicanism* (Boston: Houghton Mifflin, 2004), 207-13.

[31] Ferling, *Adams vs. Jefferson*, 200.

[32] See Peirce and Longley, *The People's President*, 41-42.

[33] Elkins and McKitrick, *Age of Federalism*, 514.

[34] Elkins and McKitrick, 693; Kuroda, *Origins of the Twelfth Amendment*, 129.

[35] Kuroda, *Origins of the Twelfth Amendment*, 119.

[36] Kuroda, chaps. 12-15; Peirce and Longley, *The People's President*, 41-44.

4. The Failures of Original Intent from the Twelfth Amendment to the Present

[1] Peirce and Longley, *The People's President*, 44-45, 247-49.

² Lawrence D. Longley and Neal R. Peirce, *The Electoral College Primer 2000* (New Haven: Yale University Press, 1999), 102.

³ Peirce and Longley, 45-47 247-49 (inconsistent as to whether Maryland had a district system in 1836); Koza, *Every Vote Equal*, 10 (§ 1.1).

⁴ Peirce and Longley, *The People's President*, 49-51.

⁵ Peirce and Longley, 49-51.

⁶ Peirce and Longley, 52-5, 242. Peirce and Longley refer to Tilden's "plurality," but the numbers they cite show that Tilden won a majority, not just a plurality, of all the popular votes, whether one accepts the Republican numbers (53), the Democratic numbers (53), or what they call the "modern-day" numerical analysis (242). Cf. Dave Leip, "1876 Presidential General Election Results," *Atlas of U.S. Presidential Elections*, accessed January 11, 2018, https://uselectionatlas.org/RESULTS/national.php?year=1876 (showing Tilden with 50.9% of the popular vote).

⁷ Peirce and Longley, *The People's President*, 57-58.

⁸ Peirce and Longley, 63-73, 284-85; Longley and Peirce, *Electoral College Primer*, 46-52.

⁹ U.S. Federal Election Commission, "2000 Official Presidential General Election Results," accessed January 11, 2018, https://transition.fec.gov/pubrec/2000presgeresults.htm.

¹⁰ John C. Fortier, "The 2000 Election," in *After the People Vote: A Guide to the Electoral College*, 3rd ed., ed. John C. Fortier (Washington, D.C.: AEI Press, 2004), chap. 8,

[11] Among the many books addressing these matters, see Jack L. Goldsmith, *The Terror Presidency: Law and Judgment Inside the Bush Administration* (New York: W. W. Norton, 2007); Stefan Halper and Jonathan Clarke, *America Alone: The Neo-Conservatives and the Global Order* (New York: Cambridge University Press, 2004); James Mann, *Rise of the Vulcans: The History of Bush's War Cabinet* (New York: Penguin Books, 2004); Ron Suskind, *The One Percent Doctrine: Deep Inside America's Pursuit of Its Enemies Since 9/11* (New York: Simon & Shuster, 2004); Ron Suskind, *The Price of Loyalty: George W. Bush, the White House, and the Education of Paul O'Neill* (New York: Simon & Shuster, 2004); Scott McClellan, *What Happened: Inside the Bush White House* (New York: PublicAffairs, 2008); and Bethany McLean and Joe Nocera, *All the Devils Are Here: The Hidden History of the Financial Crisis* (New York: Portfolio / Penguin, 2011).

[12] Keith E. Stanovich, *What Intelligence Tests Miss: The Psychology of Rational Thought* (New Haven: Yale University Press, 2009), 1-2 (quotation on p. 2), 6-7, 42-44.

[13] U.S. Federal Election Commission, "2016 Official Presidential General Election Results," accessed January 11, 2018, https://transition.fec.gov/pubrec/fe2016/2016presgeresults.pdf .

[14] Among the many sources corroborating these and related matters, see Steven Levitsky and Daniel Ziblatt, *How Democracies Die* (New York: Crown, 2018); David Frum,

Trumpocracy: The Corruption of the American Republic (New York: Harper, 2018); E. J. Dionne Jr., Norman J. Ornstein, and Thomas E. Mann, *One Nation After Trump: A Guide for the Perplexed, the Disillusioned, the Desperate, and the Not-Yet Deported* (New York: St. Martin's, 2017); Timothy Snyder, *On Tyranny: Twenty Lessons from the Twentieth Century* (New York: Tim Duggan Books, 2017); Donna Brazile, *Hacks: The Inside Story of the Break-Ins and Breakdowns That Put Donald Trump in the White House* (New York: Hachette Books, 2017); Ashley Gold, "Twitter: More Than 677,000 U.S. Users Engaged with Russian Troll Accounts," *Politico*, January 19, 2018, https://www.politico.com/story/2018/01/19/twitter-users-russian-trolls-437247; *United States of America v. Internet Research Agency, LLC*, United States District Court for the District of Columbia, Criminal Case No. _, Indictment of 13 Russian defendants, February 16, 2018, https://assets.documentcloud.org/documents/4380529/Internet-Research-Agency-Indictment.pdf; Dana Milbank, "Is Trump's Doctor Okay?," *Washington Post*, January 17, 2018, https://www.washingtonpost.com/opinions/is-trumps-doctor-okay/2018/01/17/0d887f50-fbce-11e7-ad8c-ecbb62019393_story.html?utm_term=.9b88c0efc33a; and Sean Wilentz, "They Were Bad. He May Be Worse," *New York Times*, January 20, 2018, https://www.nytimes.com/2018/01/20/opinion/sunday/trum

p-bad-presidents-history.html. As for why many longtime Democrats voted for Trump in 2016, compare Thomas Frank, *Listen Liberal: Or What Ever Happened to the Party of the People?* (New York: Metropolitan Books, 2016) with Hillary Rodham Clinton, *What Happened* (New York: Simon & Shuster, 2017). The Democratic Party is not blameless for the historical circumstances that led to Trumpist populism, but the Democratic failures mostly go back to policy decisions that were made in the presidential administration of Bill Clinton—decisions that were encouraged, aided, and abetted by congressional Republicans and Republican media.

5. Evaluations of the Current Electoral College System and Proposed Alternatives Other Than Direct Popular Vote

[1] Walter Berns, "Let's Hear It for the Electoral College," in Fortier, *After the People Vote*, 53 (italics in the original, bold emphasis added).

[2] Berns, 53-54 (italics in the original, bold emphasis added). For Storing's complete testimony, see *Toward a More Perfect Union: Writings of Herbert J. Storing*, ed. Joseph M. Bessette (Washington, D.C.: AEI Press, 1995), chap. 21.

[3] *Federalist* No. 68, March 12, 1788, *Founders Online*, National Archives, last modified June 29, 2017, https://founders.archives.gov/documents/Hamilton/01-04-02-0218 (emphasis added).

[4] Levitsky and Ziblatt, *How Democracies Die*, 40.

[5] *Federalist* No. 64, in Hamilton, Jay, and Madison, *The Federalist: Gideon Edition*, 333 (emphasis added). Jay also applied these considerations to senators, who were selected by the state legislatures in the original version of the Constitution (before the Seventeenth Amendment). I have used ellipses in the quotation to skip over the references to senators, as such language is not relevant to the issue of the Electoral College.

[6] See also, among many other books, Levitsky and Ziblatt, *How Democracies Die*, 40-41, and Robert W. Bennett, *Taming the Electoral College* (Stanford CA: Stanford Law and Politics, 2006), 45.

[7] Tara Ross, *The Indispensable Electoral College: How the Founders' Plan Saves Our Country from Mob Rule* (Washington, D.C. Regnery Gateway, 2017), esp. chap. 1; Ross, *Enlightened Democracy: The Case for the Electoral College*, 2nd ed. (Dallas, TX: Colonial Press, 2012), esp. chaps. 1 and 2. Ross has also written and published a children's book (age range 8-12, per Amazon) on the Electoral College, which I have not read and will not address.

[8] Ross, *Enlightened Democracy*, 249-50n40. Ross repeated this attack on the Seventeenth Amendment in her 2017 book. Ross, *Indispensable Electoral College*, 205-6n4.

[9] Ross, *Enlightened Democracy*, 56.

[10] *McCulloch v. Md.*, 17 U.S. 316, 406-07 (1819) (emphasis added).

[11] Hutson, *Supplement*, 183 (the language in parenthesis was crossed out in the original).

[12] R. Kent Newmyer, *John Marshall and the Heroic Age of the Supreme Court* (Baton Rouge: Louisiana State University Press, 2001), 270.

[13] Ross, *Enlightened Democracy*, 62-63 (endnotes omitted).

[14] Ross, *Indispensable Electoral College*, 205-6n4; Ross, *Enlightened Democracy*, 249-50n40.

[15] Andrew C. McLaughlin, *A Constitutional History of the United States* (1935; repr., Safety Harbor, FL: Simon Publications, 2001), 1:vii.

[16] For this and the preceding paragraphs, see, for example, James M. McPherson, *Abraham Lincoln and the Second American Revolution* (New York: Oxford University Press, 1991); Gerald N. Magliocca, *American Founding Son: John Bingham and the Invention of the Fourteenth Amendment* (New York: New York University Press, 2013); Garrett Epps, *Democracy Reborn: The Fourteenth Amendment and the Fight for Equal Rights in Post-Civil War America* (New York: Henry Holt, 2006); Michael Kent Curtis, *No State Shall Abridge: The Fourteenth Amendment and the Bill of Rights* (Durham, NC: Duke University Press, 1986); Colin Woodard, *American Character: A History of the Epic Struggle Between Individual Liberty and the Common Good* (New York: Viking, 2016); H. W. Brands, *American Colossus: The Triumph of Capitalism, 1865-1900* (New York: Doubleday, 2010); David Sehat, *The Jefferson Rule: Why We Think the*

Founding Fathers Have All the Answers (New York: Simon & Shuster, 2015); and David A. Strauss, *The Living Constitution* (New York: Oxford University Press, 2010), esp. 112-14, 131-32.

[17] Magliocca, *American Founding Son*, 1.

[18] Gordon S. Wood, *The Making of the Constitution* (Waco, TX: Baylor University Press, 1987), 19.

[19] The historical transition to the winner-take-all system magnified the large-state advantage: "The net result of the two elector 'bonus' for less populous states and the winner-take-all rule is that voters in the states with very large delegations actually cast mathematically weightier votes than do voters in other states." Bennett, *Taming the Electoral College*, 162 (endnote omitted).

[20] Madison stated on June 18, 1788, in the Virginia ratifying convention: "The Deputies from the small States [at the Constitutional Convention] argued, (and there is some force in their reasoning) that when the people [*sic*; sometimes it was the state legislatures] voted [for the electors], the large States evidently had the advantage over the rest, and without varying the mode, the interests of the little States might be neglected or sacrificed. Here is a compromise.—For in the eventual election [the House contingency election], the small States will have the advantage." *DHRC*, 10:1377, http://rotunda.upress.virginia.edu/founders/RNCN-02-10-02-0002-0007. This was, in fact, the exact argument of states' rights advocate Roger Sherman at the Constitutional Convention on September 5, 1787: "if the Small States had

the advantage in the in the [contingent election], the Large States would have in fact the nomination of these candidates [in the electoral vote preceding the contingent election]." Farrand, *Records*, 2:512-13 (Madison's notes). Massachusetts delegate Rufus King made the same point. Farrand, 2:514 (Madison's notes). Decades later, Madison wrote that "[t]he part of the arrangement which casts the eventual appointment on the [House of Representatives] voting by States, was . . . an accommodation to the anxiety of the smaller States for their sovereign equality. . . ." Madison to George Hay, August 23, 1823, *Founders Online*, National Archives, last modified June 29, 2017, https://founders.archives.gov/documents/Madison/04-03-02-0109. See also Rakove, *Original Meanings*, 90.

[21] Nathaniel Gorham in the Massachusetts ratifying convention, January 28, 1788, *DHRC*, 7:1813, http://rotunda.upress.virginia.edu/founders/RNCN-02-07-03-0001-0020 (Justus Dwight journal).

[22] For details regarding the debate over the Twelfth Amendment, see Kuroda, *Origins of the Twelfth Amendment*, chaps. 12-15.

[23] Farrand, *Records*, 1:323.

[24] James Madison to Thomas Jefferson, September 6, 1787, *Founders Online,* National Archives, last modified November 26, 2017, http://founders.archives.gov/documents/Madison/01-10-02-0115; Wood, *Making of the Constitution*, 14-20, 23-36;

Gordon S. Wood, *The Creation of the American Republic, 1776-1787* (1969; repr., Chapel Hill: University of North Carolina Press, 1998), chap. 12; Rakove, *Original Meanings*, chap. 7. As explained earlier, the nationalists at the Constitutional Convention opposed any involvement of the state legislatures in presidential elections, but they had to compromise on this point as well. Since today all states base the awards of their electoral votes on the results of the popular election in their respective states (as distinguished from direct selection of the electors by the state legislatures, which often occurred in the early decades of the republic), the current involvement of the state legislatures is limited to administrative matters.

[25] Farrand, *Records*, 1:162-63 (Journal), 164-68 (Madison's notes), 169-71 (Robert Yates's notes), 171-73 (Rufus King's notes). This was a motion by Charles Pinckney and James Madison to replace language in the pending draft constitution whereby the national legislature would have had power "to negative all laws passed by the several States, contravening, in the opinion of the national legislature the articles of union; or of any treaties subsisting under the authority of the union." Farrand, 1:162 (Journal).

[26] Farrand, 1:165 (Madison's notes).

[27] James Madison to Thomas Jefferson, October 24, 1787, *Founders Online,* National Archives, last modified November 26, 2017, http://founders.archives.gov/documents/Madison/01-10-02-

0151. See also Chapters 1-3 and the Appendix for additional discussion and documentation of the factual statements about the founding era in this and the preceding paragraphs. For further refutation of the notion that the Electoral College was designed to preserve federalism, see George C. Edwards III, *Why the Electoral College Is Bad for America* (New Haven: Yale University Press, 2004), 115-16, 119-22.

[28] Ross, *Indispensable Electoral College*, 153.

[29] See also Koza, *Every Vote Equal*, 369-73 (§ 9.1.5); Bennett, *Taming the Electoral College*, 46.

[30] See the Appendix and Chapters 1 and 2 of the present book.

[31] Ross, *Indispensable Electoral College*, 78.

[32] Ross, 78-81. Ross later says (120) that "rumors swirled that some of the protests [against Trump's election] were funded by the liberal donor George Soros." Soros is, of course the bogeyman of the right. Ross is content to repeat this right-wing meme without any attempt at corroboration. The unsubstantiated notion that anti-Trump protests were fueled by Soros's money is, in fact, risible, as anyone who has any familiarity with those protests is aware.

[33] Ross, 120.

[34] Ross, 122.

[35] Robert M. Alexander, *Presidential Electors and the Electoral College: An Examination of Lobbying, Wavering Electors, and Campaigns for Faithless Votes* (Amherst, NY: Cambria, 2012).

[36] Many supporters of the Electoral College also make arguments alleging historical expediency, some of which are self-contradictory and others of which are highly questionable as a matter of enduring historical fact. Other analysts have adequately rebutted these concrete arguments, and it is not necessary to rehearse their weaknesses again in the present book. E.g., Bennett, *Taming the Electoral College*, 58-67; Koza, *Every Vote Equal*, chap. 9 passim; Edwards, *Why the Electoral College is Bad*, chap. 5. I would add, as discussed throughout the present book, that the election of 2016 turned many of these Electoral College arguments on their head: the 2016 Electoral College winner has fulfilled the worst nightmares of the proponents of the Electoral College, including the fear of mob rule.

[37] Peirce and Longley, *The People's President*, 132-44; Longley and Peirce, *Electoral College Primer*, 106-7; Bennett, *Taming the Electoral College*, 42-44, 50-51, 130, 214n25; Paul Schumaker, "Analyzing the Electoral College and Its Alternatives," in *Choosing a President: The Electoral College and Beyond*, ed. Paul D. Schumaker and Burdett A. Loomis (New York: Seven Bridges Press, 2002), 15-16; Gary E. Bugh, "The Challenge of Contemporary Electoral College Reform," in Bugh, *Electoral College Reform*, 81; Edwards, *Why the Electoral College Is Bad*, 9-10, 34-38, 153; Ross, *Enlightened Democracy*, 143-45.

[38] Peirce and Longley, *The People's President*, 136-44; Burdett A. Loomis et al., "Electoral College Reform, the Presidency, and Congress," in Schumaker and Loomis,

Choosing a President, 79; Paul Schumaker and Burdett A. Loomis, "Reaching a Collective Judgment," in Schumaker and Loomis, *Choosing a President*, 196; Koza, *Every Vote Equal*, 141-42 (§ 3.3) (noting, *inter alia*, that Senators Robert C. Byrd of West Virginia, John Sparkman of Alabama, and John Stennis of Mississippi were sponsors of Senate Joint Resolution 12, proposing the district plan, in 1969; Byrd, Sparkman, and Stennis were, of course, conservative Democrats).

[39] Allan Cigler et al., "Changing the Electoral College: The Impact on Parties and Organized Interests," in Schumaker and Loomis, *Choosing a President*, 97; Ross, *Enlightened Democracy*, 145.

[40] Ross, *Enlightened Democracy*, 145.

[41] Koza, *Every Vote Equal*, 194-203 (§ 4.2).

[42] Bennett, *Taming the Electoral College*, 51; Cigler, 97-98; Edwards, *Why the Electoral College is Bad*, 153; Ross, *Enlightened Democracy*, 144-45.

[43] Koza, *Every Vote Equal*, 203-4 (§ 4.2.1).

[44] Peirce and Longley, *The People's President*, 138-143.

[45] Peirce and Longley, 144-56; Koza, *Every Vote Equal*, 130-41 (§ 3.2), 158-61 (§ 4.1).

[46] Peirce and Longley, *The People's President*, 144-56; Koza, *Every Vote Equal*, 130-41 (§ 3.2), 158-61 (§ 4.1), 680-86 (§ 9.23.2); Bennett, *Taming the Electoral College*, 50-53, Edwards, *Why the Electoral College is Bad*, 153; Ross, *Enlightened Democracy*, 146-47.

[47] Robert W. Bennett, Abstract, "Popular Election of the President Without a Constitutional Amendment," March 27, 2001,
https://papers.ssrn.com/sol3/papers.cfm?abstract_id=261057.

[48] Bennett, *Taming the Electoral College*, x, 170-78.

[49] Koza, *Every Vote Equal*, which can be downloaded for free at http://www.every-vote-equal.com/.

[50] Koza, 258-60 (§ 6.2), http://www.every-vote-equal.com/sites/default/files/eve-4th-ed-ch6-web-v1.pdf. The current list of state signatories is at http://www.nationalpopularvote.com/ (National Popular Vote website).

[51] Bennett, *Taming the Electoral College*, 11 (quotation), 161-78 passim; cf. Strauss, *The Living Constitution*, 132-36 (discussion of constitutional amendments ratifying changes that had already been substantially effected in an indirect manner, for example by state statutes).

[52] Ralph Z. Hallow, "RNC Stomps Electoral College Switch," *Washington Times*, August 5, 2011, https://www.washingtontimes.com/news/2011/aug/5/rnc-nixes-national-popular-vote-initiative/.

[53] Ross, *Enlightened Democracy*, chaps 12-14, Ross, *Indispensable Electoral College*, 99. The Compact Clause is in Section 10, Clause 3 of the Constitution: "No State shall, without the Consent of Congress, . . . enter into any Agreement or Compact with another State . . . ." If the National Popular Vote Compact becomes effective, it is

certain that conservatives will commence litigation alleging its unconstitutionality. Ross, *Enlightened Democracy*, 183 ("Several aspects of the NPV proposal will inevitably be the subject of litigation if a significant number of states approve the NPV compact").

6. A Proposed Constitutional Amendment for Election of the President and Vice President by Direct Popular Vote

[1] *DHRC*, 10:1412, http://rotunda.upress.virginia.edu/founders/RNCN-02-10-02-0002-0009 (dashes omitted).

[2] *DHRC*, 10:1371, http://rotunda.upress.virginia.edu/founders/RNCN-02-10-02-0002-0007. See the subsection on the Virginia ratifying convention in Chapter 2 for the context of Madison's remark.

[3] The earlier proposed amendments are contained in Koza, *Every Vote Equal*, 142-55 (§ 3.4) (http://www.every-vote-equal.com/sites/default/files/eve-4th-ed-ch3-web-v1.pdf) and Peirce and Longley, *The People's President*, 292-93.

[4] Peirce and Longley, *The People's President*, 292; Koza, *Every Vote Equal*, 142-46 (§ 3.4).

[5] "Voter Registration Age Requirements by State," USA.gov, accessed February 10, 2018, https://www.usa.gov/voter-registration-age-requirements. The Twenty-Sixth Amendment provides: "The right of citizens of the United States, who are eighteen years of age or older, to vote shall not be denied or abridged by the United States or by any State on account of age."

[6] Koza, *Every Vote Equal*, 93-95 (§ 2.4).

[7] Longley and Peirce, *Electoral College Primer*, 128-29.

[8] Bennett, *Taming the Electoral College*, 49, 209n94.

[9] Thomas E. Mann and Norman J. Ornstein, *It's Even Worse Than It Looks: How the American Constitutional System Collided With the New Politics of Extremism* (New York: Basic Books, 2012), 150.

[10] Koza, *Every Vote Equal*, 11-47, 693-96 (§§ 1.2, 1.2.1, 9.25.1); Edwards, *Why the Electoral College is Bad*, 120-21; Longley and Peirce, *Electoral College Primer*, 165-66; Matthew J. Streb, *Rethinking American Electoral Democracy*, 3rd ed. (New York: Routledge, 2016), 164-65, 169; Bennett, *Taming the Electoral College*, 163, 172.

[11] Dionne, *One Nation After Trump*, generally and 258-59 (instant runoff voting); Mann and Ornstein, *It's Even Worse Than It Looks*, 150.

[12] INSTANT RUNOFF.COM, http://instantrunoff.com/instant-runoff-home/; FairVote, http://www.fairvote.org/; Streb, *Rethinking American Electoral Democracy*, 173-74; Dionne, *One Nation After Trump*, 258-59; Mann and Ornstein, *It's Even Worse Than It Looks*, 150.

[13] Streb, *Rethinking American Electoral Democracy*, 163 (endnote omitted).

[14] Koza, *Every Vote Equal*, 586-97, 745-46 (§§ 9.15.1, 9.15.2, 9.31.12); Edwards, *Why the Electoral College is Bad*, 122-25;

Streb, *Rethinking American Electoral Democracy*, 166-67; Bennett, *Taming the Electoral College*, 65-67.

[15] Edwards, *Why the Electoral College is Bad*, 124 (italics in the original).

[16] Erik S. Herron, Ronald A. Francisco, and O. Fiona Yap, "Election Rules and Social Stability," in Schumaker and Loomis, *Choosing a President*, 156.

[17] Peirce and Longley, *The People's President*, 63-73, 284-85; Longley and Peirce, *The Electoral College Primer*, 46-52.

[18] Thus, the title of Tara Ross's latest book: *The Indispensable Electoral College: How the Founders' Plan Saves Our Country from Mob Rule*. As established in Chapter 5, the current Electoral College is definitely not "the Founders' Plan."

[19] Frum, *Trumpocracy*, 141.

[20] Streb, *Rethinking American Electoral Democracy*, 211.

[21] *DHRC*, 10:1412, http://rotunda.upress.virginia.edu/founders/RNCN-02-10-02-0002-0009 (dashes omitted).

[22] See Chapter 1 (section on "Advocates and Opponents of Direct Popular Election of the President") and Appendix passim.

Appendix. A Detailed Narrative of the Debates in the 1787 Constitutional Convention on the Selection of the President

[1] The Journal and the extant notes of the delegates are contained in Max Farrand, ed., *The Records of the Federal Convention of 1787*, 4 vols. (New Haven, CT: Yale University Press, 1966) and James H. Hutson, ed., *Supplement to Max Farrand's "The Records of the Federal Convention of 1787"* (New Haven, CT: Yale University Press, 1987). With regard to James Madison's notes, see also *Documentary History of the Constitution, 1786-1870*, vol. 3 (Washington, D.C.: Department of State, 1900) (hereafter cited as *DHC*), which Professor Mary Sarah Bilder has described as "the most accurate transcription" of Madison's notes. Bilder, *Madison's Hand: Revising the Constitutional Convention* (Cambridge, MA: Harvard University Press, 2015), 237. Although Farrand's above-referenced volumes appear to incorporate Madison's later revisions (using angle brackets to distinguish them from earlier drafts), volume 3 of the *DHC* has the virtue of reproducing in printed form the state of the manuscript (with inserted revisions) in Madison's possession at the time of his death in 1836.

As explained in the foregoing sources, Madison revised the first draft of his notes in later years and decades. Pursuant to his instructions, his notes were not published until after his death. Bilder, *Madison's Hand*, 223-240. The present book usually cites to Farrand's *Records*, because that work, with Hutson's *Supplement,* is more accessible than is the *DHC.*

Since neither Madison nor anyone else present at the Convention acted in the capacity of a stenographer, their respective notes were probably influenced, to some extent, by their own political views. See Bilder, *Madison's Hand,* for her argument to this effect. Nevertheless, these records are the next best thing to a stenographic transcript. The present account (whether in this Appendix or in the main body of the book) also occasionally cites later reminiscences of the delegates as to the Convention proceedings. Although often useful for filling in gaps left in the notes of the Convention attendees, it must be borne in mind that these later recollections may have been affected by the then current political controversies and/or the fading memories of the participants.

I sometimes paraphrase Madison's notes or other primary sources in this book. In the interest of accuracy, these paraphrases often track the primary source's language while modernizing it slightly for the twenty-first-century reader. In such cases I have not used quotation marks, because it is not an exact quotation. In all cases, however, I have cited the primary source involved. I do not utilize such close paraphrases for secondary sources. If a previously published secondary source happens to be similar in language to my paraphrases, it means that such secondary source itself employed the same procedure with regard to the primary source.

There are occasionally obvious unintentional errors in the documents, for example, the repetition of a word, a comma followed immediately by a period, or a sentence ending in a comma. In such cases I have silently corrected the document when quoting from it. Otherwise, my quotations are exact reproductions of the documents cited, with capitalization, spelling, punctuation, and so forth as in the document cited, except when I have indicated my changes in brackets. However, Madison and other writers of his era sometimes used a long dash (3-em dash in print) to end or break up a sentence. When the long dash is at the end of quoted material, I have silently converted it to a period.

[2] Letter of Several Gentlemen of Rhode Island to the Chairman of the General Convention, May 11, 1787, in Farrand, *Records*, 3:18-20.

[3] Farrand, 3:588, 590 (App. B: The Delegates to the Federal Convention, Their Credentials, and Attendance"). Cf. Max Farrand, *The Framing of the Constitution of the United States* (New Haven, CT: Yale University Press, 1913), 94.

[4] Farrand, *Records*, 1:21 (Madison's notes), 28 (William Paterson's notes); cf. Farrand, 3:593-94 (App. C: "The Virginia Plan or Randolph Resolutions"). "[T]here is little doubt that . . . the celebrated Virginia Plan presented by Governor Randolph on May 29 . . . was largely a product of

Madison's creative genius." Clinton Rossiter, *1787: The Grand Convention* (New York: W. W. Norton, 1987), 161. On October 12, 1804, Madison wrote to Noah Webster that the Virginia delegates, upon their arrival in Philadelphia, "having agreed among themselves on the outline of a plan, it was laid before the convention by Mr. Randolph...." Farrand, *Records*, 3:409. On May 25, 1826, Madison advised Andrew Stevenson that Randolph's "propositions were the result of a meeting of the whole [Virginia] Deputation, and concurred or acquiesced in unanimously, merely as a general introduction of the business...." Farrand, 3:474. In a December 1831 letter to N. P. Trist, Madison again referred to the Virginia Plan resolutions as having resulted from "a consultation among whom [the Virginia delegates] they [the resolutions] were the result." Farrand, 3:517. In an undated letter that apparently was not sent (but prepared after February 6, 1833), Madison stated that "[t]he Resolutions proposed by [Randolph] were the result of a Consultation among the [Virginia] Deputies, the whole number, seven being present.... **It was perfectly understood, that the Propositions committed no one to their precise tenor or form; and that the members of the Deputation wd. be as free in discussing and shaping them as other members of the Convention.**" Farrand, 3:525 (emphasis added). In a January 6, 1834 letter to Thomas S. Grimke, Madison observed that "[t]he propositions of Mr. Randolph were the result of a consultation among the seven Virginia Deputies, of which he, being at the time Governor of the State, was the organ. . . . **It was meant that they should sketch a real and adequate Govt. for the Union, but without committing the parties agst. a freedom in discussing & deciding on any of them.**" Farrand, 3:532 (emphasis added). Again, in a June 5, 1835 letter to W. A. Duer, Madison remarked that the Randolph resolutions "were understood **not to commit any of the members absolutely or definitively on the tenor of them.**" Farrand, 3:536 (emphasis added). Finally, in an unfinished preface to his notes of the Convention, Madison stated: "**The Resolutions introduced by Governor Randolph were the result of a Consultation on the subject; with an understanding that they left all the Deputies entirely open to the lights of discussion, and free to concur in any alternations or modifications which their reflections and judgements might approve.** *DHC* 3:796m-n (emphasis added). Farrand, 3:549, has "Consolidation" rather than "Consultation."

[5] James Madison to George Washington, April 16, 1787, *Founders Online*, National Archives, last modified June 29, 2017, https://founders.archives.gov/documents/Madison/01-09-02-0208.

[6] Farrand, *Records*, 1:29 (Journal), 33 (Madison's notes).

[7] See David O. Stewart, *The Summer of 1787: The Men Who Invented the Constitution* (New York: Simon & Schuster, 2007), 53-54.

[8] Farrand, *Records*, 1:62-63 (Journal), 64-65 (Madison's notes).

[9] Farrand, 1:66 (Madison's notes).

[10] Farrand, 1:66-69 (Madison's notes).

[11] Farrand, 1:68 (Madison's notes).

[12] Farrand, 1:68 (Madison's notes).

[13] Farrand, 1:69 (Madison's notes) (emphasis added).

[14] Farrand, 1:69 (Madison's notes).

[15] Farrand, 1:69 (Madison's notes).

[16] Farrand, 1:91 (William Pierce's notes).

[17] Farrand, 1:77 (Journal), 80 (Madison's notes).

[18] Farrand, 1:80 (Madison's notes).

[19] Farrand, 1:81 (Madison's notes), 91 (Pierce's notes).

[20] Farrand, 1:77 (Journal), 80-81 (Madison's notes).

[21] Farrand, 1:20 (Resolution 5 of the Virginia Plan).

[22] Farrand, 1:148-49 (Journal).

[23] Farrand, 1:162-63 (Journal), 164-68 (Madison's notes), 169-71 (Robert Yates's notes), 171-73 (Rufus King's notes); cf. Bilder, *Madison's Hand*, 74-77, 244-45 (arguing that Madison later replaced his speeches of this date and that the extant version is not the original).

[24] Farrand, *Records*, 1:163 (Journal), 168 (Madison's notes).

[25] Farrand, 1:174-75 (Journal), 175-76 (Madison's notes), 180-81 (Yates's notes).

[26] Farrand, 1:176 (Madison's notes), 180-81 (Yates's notes); see also Farrand, 1:174-75 (Journal).

[27] Farrand, 1:225-26, 230 (Journal), 236 (Madison's notes).

[28] Farrand, 1:240 (Journal, Madison's notes, Yates's notes).

[29] Farrand, 1:242 (Journal), 242-45 (Madison's notes), 246 (Yates's notes), 247 (King's notes); cf. Farrand, 3:611-16 (App. E: "The New Jersey Plan or Paterson Resolutions").

[30] Farrand, 1:283-93 (Madison's notes), 294-301 (Yates's notes), 304-11 (Hamilton's Notes).

[31] Farrand, 1:590-91 (Journal), 597 (Madison's notes). For a discussion of these developments in the Convention, see Lawrence Goldstone, *Dark Bargain: Slavery, Profits, and the Struggle for the Constitution* (New York: Bloomsbury, 2005), Kindle ed., chap. 11.

[32] Farrand, *Records*, 2:13-15, 84 (Journal); 15-20, 87 (Madison's notes). For a general discussion of the Great Compromise, see Farrand, *Framing of the Constitution*, chap. 7.

[33] Farrand, *Records*, 1:229 (Journal), 236 (Madison's notes); 2:21-22 (Journal), 27-28 (Madison's notes).

[34] Farrand, 2:28-29 (Madison's notes).

[35] Farrand, 2:22 (Journal), 29 (Madison's notes).

[36] Farrand, 2:22, 24 (Journal), 32 (Madison's notes).

[37] Farrand, 2:29 (Madison's notes) (emphasis added).

[38] Farrand, 2:29 (Madison's notes).

[39] Farrand, 2:29-30 (Madison's notes).

[40] Farrand, 2:30 (Madison's notes).

[41] Farrand, 2:30-31 (Madison's notes).

[42] Farrand, 2:31 (Madison's notes).

[43] Farrand, 2:31 (Madison's notes).

[44] Farrand, 2:32 (Madison's notes).

[45] Farrand, 2:22, 24 (Journal), 32 (Madison's notes). New Hampshire, New York, and Rhode Island were all absent from voting that day, so there were only ten states voting on these measures.

[46] Akhil Reed Amar, *America's Constitution: A Biography* (New York: Random House, 2005), 157.

[47] Farrand, *Records*, 2:22, 24 (Journal), 32 (Madison's notes).

[48] Farrand, 2: 22, 24 (Journal), 32 (Madison's notes).

[49] Farrand, 2:52-54 (Madison's notes) (emphasis added).

[50] Farrand, 2:54-55 (Madison's notes).

[51] Farrand, 2:55-56 (Madison's notes).

[52] Farrand, 2:56 (Madison's notes).

[53] Farrand, 2:56 (Madison's notes) (emphasis added).

[54] "Although [Madison] had [presumably] favored an elective tenure for the executive in the Virginia plan [wherein the executive was to be elected by the national legislature], his anxiety about an executive dependent on a legislature controlled by small states may have been overwhelming." Bilder, *Madison's Hand*, 115.

[55] Farrand, *Records*, 2:56-57 (Madison's notes, emphasis added).

[56] See David Waldstreicher, *Slavery's Constitution: From Revolution to Ratification* (New York: Hill and Wang, 2010), 89.

[57] Goldstone, *Dark Bargain*, chap. 13 (third paragraph), Kindle loc. 2477-83.

[58] Farrand, *Records*, 2:60-63 (Journal), 64 (Madison's notes).

[59] Farrand, 2:57 (Madison's notes) (emphasis added).

[60] Farrand, 2:57 (Madison's notes).

[61] Farrand, 2:63 (Madison's notes).

[62] Farrand, 2:50 (Journal), 58 (Madison's notes).

[63] Farrand 2:57 (Madison's notes).

[64] Farrand, 2:50-51 (Journal), 57-59 (Madison's notes).

[65] Farrand, 2:60-62 (Journal), 64 (Madison's notes).

[66] Farrand, 2:71 (Journal), 73 (Madison's notes).

[67] Farrand, 2:85 (Journal), 87 (Madison's notes); 3:61 (Hugh Williamson to James Iredell, July 22, 1787).

[68] Farrand, 2:62, 72, 86, 98 (Journal), 95 (Madison's notes, referring to ten states present on July 23). Two of the three New York delegates, John Lansing and Robert Yates, had left the Convention on July 10, and the third, Alexander Hamilton, had left on June 29. Farrand, 3:588, 590 (App. B).

[69] Farrand, 2:85-87 (Journal), 95-96 (Madison's notes).

[70] Farrand, 2:97-98 (Journal), 99-106 (Madison's notes).

[71] Farrand, 2:107 (Journal), 108-11 (Madison's notes).

[72] Farrand, 2:107-8 (Journal), 109 (Madison's notes).

[73] Farrand, 2:109-10 (Madison's notes) (emphasis added).

[74] Farrand, 2:110 (Madison's notes).

[75] Farrand, 2:110-11 (Madison's notes).

[76] Madison had crossed out "freeholders" and substituted "qualified part of them ...." Farrand, 2:111. At that time different states had different qualifications for the franchise.

In addition to the fact that women and slaves could not vote, states also had property qualifications for voting.

[77] Farrand, 2:111 (Madison's notes) (emphasis added).

[78] Farrand, 2:111 (Madison's notes).

[79] Farrand, 2:111-12 (Madison's notes).

[80] Farrand, 2:112 (Madison's notes).

[81] Farrand, 2:112 (Madison's notes).

[82] Farrand, 2:112 (Madison's notes).

[83] Farrand, 2:112-13 (Madison's notes).

[84] Farrand, 2:103 (Madison's notes).

[85] Farrand, 2:113 (Madison's notes).

[86] Farrand, 2:114 (Madison's notes).

[87] Farrand, 2:114 (Madison's notes).

[88] See Joseph J. Ellis, *His Excellency: George Washington* (New York: Alfred A. Knopf, 2004), Kindle ed., Kindle loc. 2811-60, 3074-78; Rossiter, *1787*, 44-45; Stewart, *The Summer of 1787*, 27, 27-28, 82-83; Gordon S. Wood, *The Creation of the American Republic, 1776-1787* (Chapel Hill, NC: University of North Carolina Press, 1998), 399-400; Wood, *Empire of Liberty: A History of the Early Republic* (New York: Oxford University Press, 2009), 54, 108-9; Stanley Elkins and Eric McKitrick, *The Age of Federalism* (New York: Oxford University Press, 1993), 43.

[89] Farrand, *Records*, 2:114-15 (Madison's notes) (emphasis added).

[90] Farrand, 2:107-8 (Journal), 115 (Madison's notes).

[91] Farrand, 2:116, 118 (Journal), 118-20 (Madison's notes).

[92] Farrand, 2:116, 118 (Journal), 120-21 (Madison's notes).

[93] Farrand, 2:117-18 (Journal), 121 (Madison's notes).

[94] Farrand, 2:176 (Journal), 177-89 (Madison's notes).

[95] Farrand, 2:185 (Madison's notes).

[96] Farrand, 2:176 (Journal), 177, 189 (Madison's notes).

[97] Farrand, 2:196-97 (Madison's notes regarding the joint ballot issue).

[98] Bilder, *Madison's Hand*, 141. *Pace* Bilder's assertion that "[i]f Madison gave lengthy speeches, he kept no record," see Madison's lengthy notes of what he described as a speech giving "a pretty full view of the subject" on August 29. Farrand, *Records*, 2:451-52.

[99] Bilder, *Madison's Hand*, 141. See chapters 7 and 8 of *Madison's Hand* for an elaboration of the evidence supporting Bilder's thesis; see also 246-48.

[100] Bilder, 246-48.

[101] Bilder, 247.

[102] Farrand, *Records*, 2:401 (Madison's notes).

[103] Farrand, 2:401 (Madison's notes).

[104] Farrand, 2:401 (Madison's notes).

[105] Farrand, 2:401 (Madison's notes).

[106] Farrand, 2:401-2 (Madison's notes) (emphasis in the original).

[107] Farrand, 2:402 (Madison's notes).

[108] Farrand, 2:402 (Madison's notes) (emphasis in the original).

[109] Farrand, 2:402 (Madison's notes).

[110] Farrand, 2:402 (Madison's notes).

[111] Farrand, 2:402 (Madison's notes).

[112] Farrand, 2:402 (Madison's notes).

[113] Farrand, 2:403 (Madison's notes) (emphasis in the original).

[114] Farrand, 2:397, 399 (Journal), 403 (Madison's notes). Connecticut, New Jersey, Maryland, and Georgia voted "no." Farrand, 2:399 (Journal), 403 (Madison's notes).

[115] Farrand, 2:397, 399 (Journal), 403 (Madison's notes).

[116] Farrand, 2:397, 399 (Journal), 403 (Madison's notes).

[117] Farrand, 2:397 (Journal), 403 (Madison's notes) (the quotation is from Madison's notes, though the language of the motion was also stated in the Journal; Madison may have copied the language of the motion from the Journal).

[118] Farrand, 2:403-4 (Madison's notes). The notes of Maryland delegate James McHenry provide some additional information about Gouverneur Morris's speech. Farrand, 407 (McHenry's notes).

[119] Farrand, 2:397, 399 (Journal), 404 (Madison's notes).

[120] Farrand, 2:397, 399 (Journal), 404 (Madison's notes).

[121] Farrand, 2:397, 399 (Journal), 104 (Madison's notes). New Jersey, Pennsylvania, Delaware, and Virginia voted in favor of the motion, while New Hampshire, North Carolina, South Carolina, and Georgia voted against it.

[122] Farrand, 2:397-98 (Journal), 404 (Madison's notes).

[123] Farrand, 2:473 (Journal), 481 (Madison's notes).

[124] Farrand, 2:493-95 (Journal), 496-99 (Madison's notes).

[125] Farrand, 2:493-94 (Journal), 497-98 (Madison's notes) (emphasis added).

[126] John Dickinson to George Logan, January 16, 1802, *ConSource*, http://www.consource.org/document/john-dickinson-to-george-logan-1802-1-16/ (italic emphasis as in the original, bold emphasis added); cf. Hutson, *Supplement*, 300-301. See the section entitled "The Evolution of the Electoral College" of Chapter 1 of this book for an excerpt from this letter explaining how the change regarding the selection of the president occurred.

[127] Farrand, *Records*, 2:499 (Madison's notes).

[128] Farrand, 2:499 (Madison's notes).

[129] Farrand, 2:500 (Madison's notes).

[130] Farrand, 2:500 (Madison's notes).

[131] Farrand, 2:500 (Madison's notes).

[132] Farrand, 2:500 (Madison's notes) (emphasis added).

[133] Farrand, 2:500 (Madison's notes).

[134] Farrand, 2:501 (Madison's notes).

[135] Farrand, 2:501 (Madison's notes).

[136] Farrand, 2:501 (Madison's notes) (emphasis in the original).

[137] Farrand, 2:501 (Madison's notes).

[138] Farrand, 2:501 (Madison's notes).

[139] Farrand, 2:501-2 (Madison's notes) (emphasis added).

[140] Farrand, 2:502 (Madison's notes) (emphasis in the original).

[141] Farrand, 2:502 (Madison's notes) (emphasis in the original).

[142] Farrand, 2:511 (Madison's notes).

[143] Farrand, 2:511 (Madison's notes).

[144] Farrand, 2:507-8 (Journal), 511 (Madison's notes).

[145] Farrand, 2:512 (Madison's notes).

[146] Farrand, 2:512 (Madison's notes).

[147] Farrand, 2:512 (Madison's notes).

[148] Farrand, 2:512 (Madison's notes).

[149] Farrand, 2:512-13 (Madison's notes).

[150] Farrand, 2:507-8 (Journal), 513 (Madison's notes).

[151] Farrand, 2:507-8 (Journal), 513 (Madison's notes).

[152] Farrand, 2:513 (Madison's notes) (emphasis added).

[153] Farrand, 2:513 (Madison's notes).

[154] Farrand, 2:513 (Madison's notes).

[155] Farrand, 2:507-8 (Journal), 513 (Madison's notes).

[156] Farrand, 2:514 (Madison's notes).

[157] Farrand, 2:514 (Madison's notes).

[158] Farrand, 2:514 (Madison's notes).

[159] Farrand, 2:507-8 (Journal), 514 (Madison's notes).

[160] Farrand, 2:514 (Madison's notes). Gerry's suggestion evidently was not put in the form of a motion, or, if it was, it

was not seconded. There is no other reference to it in the Convention records.

[161] Farrand, 2:514 (Madison's notes).

[162] Farrand, 2:514 (Madison's notes).

[163] Farrand, 2:514 (Madison's notes).

[164] Farrand, 2:507-8 (Journal), 515 (Madison's notes).

[165] Farrand, 2:507-8 (Journal), 515 (Madison's notes).

[166] Farrand, 2:507-8 (Journal), 515 (Madison's notes).

[167] Farrand, 2:507-8 (Journal), 515 (Madison's notes).

[168] Farrand, 2:515 (Madison's notes).

[169] Farrand, 2:515 (Madison's notes).

[170] Farrand, 2:517 (Journal), 521 (Madison's notes).

[171] Farrand, 2:522 (Madison's notes).

[172] Farrand, 2:522 (Madison's notes).

[173] Farrand, 2:522 (Madison's notes).

[174] Farrand, 2:522 (Madison's notes).

[175] Farrand, 2:522 (Madison's notes).

[176] Farrand, 2:522 (Madison's notes).

[177] Farrand, 2:522-23 (Madison's notes).

[178] Farrand, 2:523-24 (Madison's notes).

[179] Farrand, 2:524 (Madison's notes).

[180] Farrand, 2:524 (Madison's notes).

[181] Farrand, 2:524-25 (Madison's notes).

[182] Farrand, 2:531 (McHenry's notes).

[183] Farrand, 2:517, 520 (Journal), 525 (Madison's notes).

[184] Farrand, 2:517, 520 (Journal), 525 (Madison's notes).

[185] Farrand, 2:526 (Madison's notes).

[186] Farrand, 2:518 (Journal), 526 (Madison's notes).

[187] Farrand, 2:527 (Madison's notes) (emphasis in the original).

[188] Farrand, 2:519, 520 (Journal), 527 (Madison's notes). The word "immediately" had been added to the quoted language earlier in this session.

[189] Farrand, 2:547 (Journal), 553 (Madison's notes). In the twentieth century, editor Max Farrand compiled a document corresponding to the decisions of the Convention that had been made up to this point in time. Farrand, 2:565-80 (the provisions on the selection of the president are at 572-73).

[190] Farrand, 2:582 (Journal), 585 (Madison's notes), 590-603 (Report of the Committee of Style).

[191] Farrand, 2:622 (Journal), 633 (Madison's notes).

[192] John Lienhard, "Engrossed in the Constitution," Engines of Our Ingenuity (website), no. 1003, accessed August 28, 2017, http://www.uh.edu/engines/epi1003.htm.

[193] Farrand, *Records*, 2:641 (Journal), 648-49 (Madison's notes).

[194] Farrand, 2:657-58. The conventional arabic numbering of the clauses (paragraphs) has been added for ease of reference.

ABBREVIATIONS

DHC

U.S. Department of State, ed. *Documentary History of the Constitution, 1786-1870.* Vol. 3. Washington, D.C.: Department of State, 1900.

DHRC

Kaminski, John P., Gaspare J. Saladino, Richard Leffler, Charles H. Schoenleber, and Margaret A. Hogan, eds. *The Documentary History of the Ratification of the Constitution Digital Edition.* Charlottesville: University of Virginia Press, 2009-
. http://rotunda.upress.virginia.edu/founders/RNCN.html.

Federalist

Hamilton, Alexander, John Jay, and James Madison, *The Federalist* (1787-88). Citations to the essays of Alexander Hamilton and James Madison are to *Founders Online.* Other citations are to Hamilton, Jay, and Madison, *The Federalist: The Gideon Edition,* ed. George W. Carey and James McClellan (1818; repr., Indianapolis: Liberty Fund, 2001).

Founders Online

U.S. National Archives and Records Administration, ed. *Founders Online: Correspondence and Other Writings of Six Major Shapers of the United States.* https://founders.archives.gov/.

BIBLIOGRAPHY

Adams, Willi Paul. *The First American Constitutions: Republican Ideology and the Making of the State Constitutions in the Revolutionary Era.* Expanded ed. Trans. Rita and Robert Kimber. Lanham, MD: Madison House, 2001.

Alexander, Robert M. *Presidential Electors and the Electoral College: An Examination of Lobbying, Wavering Electors, and Campaigns for Faithless Votes.* Amherst, NY: Cambria Press, 2012.

Amar, Akhil Reed. *America's Constitution: A Biography.* New York: Random House Trade Paperbacks, 2006.

Banning, Lance, ed. *Liberty and Order: The First American Party Struggle.* Indianapolis: Liberty Fund, 2004.

Beeman, Richard. *Plain, Honest Men: The Making of the American Constitution.* New York: Random House, 2010.

Bennett, Robert W. Abstract. "Popular Election of the President Without a Constitutional Amendment." March 27, 2001. https://papers.ssrn.com/sol3/papers.cfm?abstract_id=261057.

Bennett, Robert W. *Taming the Electoral College.* Stanford CA: Stanford Law and Politics, 2006.

Berns, Walter. "Let's Hear It for the Electoral College." In Fortier, *After the People Vote*, chap. 9.

Bilder, Mary Sarah. *Madison's Hand: Revising the Constitutional Convention.* Cambridge, MA: Harvard University Press, 2015.

Brands, H. W. *American Colossus: The Triumph of Capitalism, 1865-1900*. New York: Doubleday, 2010.

Bugh, Gary E. "The Challenge of Contemporary Electoral College Reform." In Bugh, *Electoral College Reform*, chap. 5.

Bugh, Gary E., ed. *Electoral College Reform: Challenges and Possibilities*. New York: Routledge, [2010], 2016.

Bugh, Gary E. "Representation in Congressional Efforts to Amend the Presidential Election System." In Bugh, *Electoral College Reform*, chap. 1.

Chernow, Ron. *Alexander Hamilton*. New York: Penguin, 2004.

Cigler, Allan, Joel Paddock, Gary Reich, and Eric Uslaner. "Changing the Electoral College: The Impact on Parties and Organized Interests." In Schumaker and Loomis, *Choosing a President*, chap. 6.

Clinton, Hillary Rodham. *What Happened*. New York: Simon & Shuster, 2017.

Collier, Christopher, and James Lincoln Collier. *Decision in Philadelphia: The Constitutional Convention of 1787*. New York: Ballantine Books, 1986.

ConSource: The Constitutional Sources Project (website). http://blog.consource.org/.

Currie, David P. *The Constitution in Congress: The Federalist Period, 1789-1801*. Chicago: University of Chicago Press, 1997.

Curtis, Michael Kent. *No State Shall Abridge: The Fourteenth Amendment and the Bill of Rights*. Durham, NC: Duke University Press, 1986.

Diamond, Martin. "The Electoral College and the American Idea of Democracy." Chap. 11 in *As Far as Republican Principles Will Admit: Essays by Martin Diamond*. Edited by William A. Schambra. Washington, D.C.: AEI Press, 1992.

Dionne, E. J., Jr., Norman J. Ornstein, and Thomas E. Mann. *One Nation After Trump: A Guide for the Perplexed, the Disillusioned, the Desperate, and the Not-Yet Deported*. New York: St. Martin's Press, 2017.

Dunn, Susan. *Jefferson's Second Revolution: The Election Crisis of 1800 and the Triumph of Republicanism*. Boston: Houghton Mifflin, 2004.

Edwards, George C., III. *Why the Electoral College Is Bad for America*. New Haven: Yale University Press, 2004.

Elkins, Stanley, and Eric McKitrick. *The Age of Federalism: The Early American Republic,, 1788-1800*. New York: Oxford University Press, 1993.

Elliot, Jonathan, ed. *The Debates in the Several State Conventions of the Adoption of the Federal Constitution as Recommended by the General Convention at Philadelphia in 1787*. 2nd ed. vol. 4. Philadelphia: J. B. Lippincott, 1866.

Ellis, Joseph J. *His Excellency: George Washington*. New York: Random House, 2004.

Epps, Garrett. *Democracy Reborn: The Fourteenth Amendment and the Fight for Equal Rights in Post-Civil War America*. New York: Henry Holt, 2006.

FairVote (website). http://www.fairvote.org/.

Farrand, Max. *The Framing of the Constitution of the United States*. New Haven: Yale University Press, 1913.

Farrand, Max, ed. *The Records of the Federal Convention of 1787*. Rev. ed. 4 vols. New Haven: Yale University Press, 1966.

Ferling, John. *Adams vs. Jefferson: The Tumultuous Election of 1800*. New York: Oxford University Press, 2004.

Ferling, John. *John Adams: A Life*. 1992; repr., New York: Owl Books, 1996.

Fortier, John C., "The 2000 Election." In Fortier, *After the People Vote*, chap. 8.

Fortier, John C., ed. *After the People Vote: A Guide to the Electoral College*. 3rd ed. Washington, D.C.: AEI Press, 2004.

Frank, Thomas. *Listen Liberal: Or What Ever Happened to the Party of the People?* New York: Metropolitan Books, 2016.

Frum, David. *Trumpocracy: The Corruption of the American Republic*. New York: Harper, 2018.

Gales, Joseph, Sr., ed. *Annals of Congress* (*The Debates and Proceedings in the Congress of the United States*). Vol. 1. Washington: Gales & Seaton, 1834. https://memory.loc.gov/cgi-bin/ampage?collId=llac&fileName=001/llac001.db&recNum=0.

Gold, Ashley. "Twitter: More Than 677,000 U.S. Users Engaged with Russian Troll Accounts." *Politico*. January 19, 2018. https://www.politico.com/story/2018/01/19/twitter-users-russian-trolls-437247.

Goldsmith, Jack L. *The Terror Presidency: Law and Judgment Inside the Bush Administration*. New York: W. W. Norton, 2007.

Goldstone, Lawrence. *Dark Bargain: Slavery, Profits, and the Struggle for the Constitution*. New York: Bloomsbury, 2005.

Hallow, Ralph Z. "RNC Stomps Electoral College Switch." *Washington Times*. August 5, 2011. https://www.washingtontimes.com/news/2011/aug/5/rnc-nixes-national-popular-vote-initiative/.

Halper, Stefan, and Jonathan Clarke. *America Alone: The Neo-Conservatives and the Global Order*. New York: Cambridge University Press, 2004.

Halperin, Terri Diane. *The Alien and Sedition Acts of 1800: Testing the Constitution*. Baltimore, Johns Hopkins Press, 2016.

Hamilton, Alexander, John Jay, and James Madison. *The Federalist: The Gideon Edition*. Edited by George W. Carey. Indianapolis, Liberty Fund, 2001. First published as separate newspaper articles 1787-88.

Herron, Erik S., Ronald A. Francisco, and O. Fiona Yap. "Election Rules and Social Stability." In Schumaker and Loomis, *Choosing a President*, chap. 10.

Hutson, James H., ed. *Supplement to Max Farrand's "The Records of the Federal Convention of 1787."* New Haven: Yale University Press, 1987.

INSTANT RUNOFF.COM (website). http://instantrunoff.com/instant-runoff-home/.

Jensen, Merrill . *The Articles of Confederation: An Interpretation of the Social-Constitutional History of the*

American Revolution, 1774-1781. 1940; repr., Madison: University of Wisconsin Press, 1966.

Kaminski, John P., and Richard Leffler, eds. *Federalists and Antifederalists: The Debate over the Ratification of the Constitution.* 2nd ed. Lanham, MD: Madison House, 1998.

Kaminski, John P., Gaspare J. Saladino, Richard Leffler, Charles H. Schoenleber, and Margaret A. Hogan, eds. *The Documentary History of the Ratification of the Constitution Digital Edition.* Charlottesville: University of Virginia Press, 2009- . http://rotunda.upress.virginia.edu/founders/RNCN.html. (Cited as *DHRC*.)

Koza, John R., Barry F. Fadem, Mark Grueskin, Michael S. Mandell, Robert Richie, and Joseph F. Zimmerman. *Every Vote Equal: A State-Based Plan for Electing the President by National Popular Vote.* 4th ed. Los Altos, CA: National Popular Vote Press, 2013.

Klein, Christopher. "The State Where Women Voted Long Before the Nineteenth Amendment." August 26, 2015. *History.* http://www.history.com/news/the-state-where-women-voted-long-before-the-19th-amendment.

Kuroda, Tadahisa. *The Origins of the Twelfth Amendment: The Electoral College in the Early Republic, 1787-1804.* Westport, CT: Greenwood Press, 1994.

Leip, Dave. "1876 Presidential General Election Results." *Atlas of U.S. Presidential Elections.* https://uselectionatlas.org/RESULTS/national.php?year=1876.

Levitsky, Steven, and Daniel Ziblatt. *How Democracies Die.* New York: Crown, 2018.

Lienhard, John. "Engrossed in the Constitution." Engines of Our Ingenuity (website). No. 1003. http://www.uh.edu/engines/epi1003.htm.

Longley, Lawrence D., and Neal R. Peirce. *The Electoral College Primer 2000.* New Haven: Yale University Press, 1999.

Loomis, Burdett A., Jeffrey Cohen, Bruce I. Oppenheimer, and James P. Pfiffner. "Electoral College Reform, the Presidency, and Congress." In Schumaker and Loomis, *Choosing a President*, chap. 5.

Magliocca, Gerald N. *American Founding Son: John Bingham and the Invention of the Fourteenth Amendment.* New York: New York University Press, 2013.

McClellan, Scott. *What Happened: Inside the Bush White House.* New York: PublicAffairs, 2008.

McCulloch v. Md., 17 U.S. 316 (1819).

McLaughlin, Andrew C. *The Confederation and the Constitution, 1783-1789.* New York: Collier Books, 1962.

McLaughlin, Andrew C. *A Constitutional History of the United* States. 1935; repr., Safety Harbor, FL: Simon Publications, 2001.

McLean, Bethany, and Joe Nocera. *All the Devils Are Here: The Hidden History of the Financial Crisis.* New York: Portfolio / Penguin, 2011.

McPherson, James M. *Abraham Lincoln and the Second American Revolution.* New York: Oxford University Press, 1991.

Maier, Pauline. *Ratification: The People Debate the Constitution, 1787-1788*. New York: Simon & Schuster, 2011.

Mann, James. *Rise of the Vulcans: The History of Bush's War Cabinet*. New York: Penguin Books, 2004.

Mann, Thomas E., and Norman J. Ornstein. *It's Even Worse Than It Looks: How the American Constitutional System Collided With the New Politics of Extremism*. New York: Basic Books, 2012.

Milbank, Dana. "Is Trump's Doctor Okay?" *Washington Post*. January 17, 2018. https://www.washingtonpost.com/opinions/is-trumps-doctor-okay/2018/01/17/0d887f50-fbce-11e7-ad8c-ecbb62019393_story.html?utm_term=.9b88c0efc33a.

Morris, Richard B. *The Forging of the Union, 1781-1789*. New York: Harper & Row, 1987.

National Popular Vote (website). https://www.nationalpopularvote.com/.

Nevins, Allan. *The American States During and After the Revolution, 1775-1789*. 1924; repr., New York: Augustus M. Kelley, 1969.

Newmyer, R. Kent. *John Marshall and the Heroic Age of the Supreme Court*. Baton Rouge: Louisiana State University Press, 2001.

Peirce, Neal R., and Lawrence D. Longley. *The People's President: The Electoral College in American History and the Direct Vote Alternative*. Rev. ed. New Haven: Yale University Press, 1981.

Rakove, Jack N. *Original Meanings: Politics and Ideas in the Making of the Constitution.* New York: Vintage Books, 1996.

Ross, Tara. *Enlightened Democracy: The Case for the Electoral College.* 2nd ed. Dallas, TX: Colonial Press, 2012.

Ross, Tara. *The Indispensable Electoral College: How the Founders' Plan Saves Our Country from Mob Rule.* Washington, D.C.: Regnery Gateway, 2017.

Rossiter, Clinton. *1787: The Grand Convention.* New York: W. W. Norton, 1987.

Schumaker, Paul D. "Analyzing the Electoral College and Its Alternatives." In Schumaker and Loomis, *Choosing a President*, chap. 2.

Schumaker, Paul D., and Burdett A. Loomis, eds. *Choosing a President: The Electoral College and Beyond.* New York: Seven Bridges Press, 2002.

Schumaker, Paul D., and Burdett A. Loomis. "Reaching a Collective Judgment." In Schumaker and Loomis, *Choosing a President*, chap. 12.

Schwartz, Bernard. *The Great Rights of Mankind: A History of the American Bill of Rights.* Expanded ed. Madison, WI: Madison House, 1992.

Sehat, David. *The Jefferson Rule: Why We Think the Founding Fathers Have All the* Answers. New York: Simon & Shuster, 2015.

Sharp, James Roger. *American Politics in the Early Republic: The New Nation in Crisis.* New Haven: Yale University Press, 1993.

Smith, Charles Page. *James Wilson, Founding Father, 1742-1798.* Chapel Hill, NC: University of North Carolina Press, 1956.

Snyder, Timothy. *On Tyranny: Twenty Lessons from the Twentieth Century.* New York: Tim Duggan Books, 2017.

Stanovich, Keith E. *What Intelligence Tests Miss: The Psychology of Rational Thought.* New Haven: Yale University Press, 2009.

Stewart, David O. *The Summer of 1787.* New York: Simon & Schuster, 2007.

Storing, Herbert. "In Defense of the Electoral College." Chap. 21 in *Toward a More Perfect Union: Writings of Herbert J. Storing.* Edited by Joseph M. Bessette. Washington, D.C.: AEI Press, 1995.

Strauss, David A. *The Living Constitution.* New York: Oxford University Press, 2010.

Streb, Matthew J. *Rethinking American Electoral Democracy.* 3rd ed. New York: Routledge, 2016.

Suskind, Ron. *The One Percent Doctrine: Deep Inside America's Pursuit of Its Enemies Since 9/11.* New York: Simon & Shuster, 2004.

Suskind, Ron. *The Price of Loyalty: George W. Bush, the White House, and the Education of Paul O'Neill.* New York: Simon & Shuster, 2004.

United States of America v. Internet Research Agency, LLC. United States District Court for the District of Columbia. Criminal Case No. _. Indictment of 13 Russian defendants. February 16, 2018. https://assets.documentcloud.org/documents/4380529/Internet-Research-Agency-Indictment.pdf.

U.S. Department of State, ed. *Documentary History of the Constitution, 1786-1870.* Vol. 3. Washington, D.C.: Department of State, 1900. (Cited as *DHC*.)

U.S. Federal Election Commission. "2000 Official Presidential General Election Results." https://transition.fec.gov/pubrec/2000presgeresults.htm.

U.S. Federal Election Commission. "2016 Official Presidential General Election Results." https://transition.fec.gov/pubrec/fe2016/2016presgeresults.pdf.

U.S. Library of Congress, ed. *Journals of the Continental Congress, 1774-1789.* Vol. 33. Washington D.C.: U.S. Government Printing Office, 1936. https://memory.loc.gov/cgi-bin/query/r?ammem/hlaw:@field(DOCID+@lit(jc0331)).

U.S. National Archives and Records Administration, ed. *Founders Online: Correspondence and Other Writings of Six Major Shapers of the United States.* https://founders.archives.gov/.

Van Cleve, George William. *A Slaveholders' Union: Slavery, Politics, and the Constitution in the Early American Republic.* Chicago: University of Chicago Press, 2010.

"Voter Registration Age Requirements by State." USA.gov. https://www.usa.gov/voter-registration-age-requirements.

Waldstreicher, David. *Slavery's Constitution: From Revolution to Ratification.* New York: Hill and Wang, 2010.

Weisberger, Bernard A. *America Afire: Jefferson, Adams, and the First Contested Election.* New York: Perennial, 2001.

Wilentz, Sean. "They Were Bad. He May Be Worse." *New York Times.* January 20, 2018. https://www.nytimes.com/2018/01/20/opinion/sunday/trump-bad-presidents-history.html.

Wood, Gordon S. *The Creation of the American Republic, 1776-1787.* 1969; repr., Chapel Hill: University of North Carolina Press, 1998.

Wood, Gordon S. *Empire of Liberty: A History of the Early Republic.* New York: Oxford University Press, 2009.

Wood, Gordon S. *The Making of the Constitution.* Waco, TX: Baylor University Press, 1987.

Woodard, Colin. *American Character: A History of the Epic Struggle Between Individual Liberty and the Common Good.* New York: Viking, 2016.

INDEX

About the Author

Alan E. Johnson is the author of *The First American Founder: Roger Williams and Freedom of Conscience* and other publications in the fields of history, constitutional law, political science, and philosophy. He is retired from a long career as an attorney in which he focused primarily, though not exclusively, on constitutional and public law litigation. He holds an A.B. (Political Science) and an A.M. (Humanities) from the University of Chicago and a J.D. from Cleveland-Marshall College of Law, Cleveland State University. For additional information and selected publications, see his website at https://alanjohnson.academia.edu/.

Made in the USA
Lexington, KY
10 March 2018